W9-DFL-071

# CONTEMPORARY CELEBRATION

# ROSS SNYDER

UNITY SCHOOL LIBRARY
UNITY VILLAGE, MISSOURI 64065

**WITHDRAWN**
by Unity Library

ABINGDON PRESS    Nashville and New York

CONTEMPORARY CELEBRATION

*Copyright © 1971 by Abingdon Press*

All rights in this book are reserved.
No part of the book may be reproduced in any
manner whatsoever without written permission of
the publishers except brief quotations embodied in
critical articles or reviews. For information address
Abingdon Press, Nashville, Tennessee.

*ISBN 0-687-0997-6*

*Library of Congress Catalog Card Number: 74-162458*

Scripture quotations noted RSV are from the Revised Standard Version of the
Bible, copyrighted 1946 and 1952 by the Division of Christian Education,
National Council of Churches, and are used by permission.

Scripture quotations noted NEB are from the New English Bible, © the
Delegates of the Oxford University Press and the Syndics of the Cambridge
University Press 1961, 1970. Reprinted by permission.

SET UP, PRINTED, AND BOUND BY THE
PARTHENON PRESS, AT NASHVILLE,
TENNESSEE, UNITED STATES OF AMERICA

To My Mother
Flossie Winifred Ross
who all the years of her life
has felt that church affairs should *move*

# Preface

Communal celebration is an aspect of every consummated length of living or learning.

Group enterprises and family life lose much of their about-to-be-interiorized treasures if there is no folk art of celebration. Public-school education is dull and flat without it. Celebration is as important a part of any humane course in a school as is solving problems or cognitive imprinting—and infinitely more important than piling up more information. A resource for teachers who believe in such new horizons for education could be helpful. Perhaps especially for all teachers of literature, human development, history, music and the arts.

For untold centuries the major instruments of communal celebration have been the religious institutions of a society. Therefore I am passionately concerned that this book contribute to intensifying realness, immediacy, presence, warmth, momentum, expectancy and surprise and astonishment and awe in church events.

For all these reasons, the time has come to develop the art-science of constructing contemporary celebrations. To lay out with considerable fullness the working capital we need if we are to develop significant communal celebration. And teach many people the forming theories and skills so that more people can get in on the act.

Communal celebration is the culminating art of all arts. We are just beginning to realize the fact. We now have—in every congregation, school, and community—many people with the necessary skills and depth of experiences—if only we open up to them the possibility in some workable design and common understanding of what contemporary communal celebration is.

A celebration is not something which rightly one person can put together. We need a team. We need books and conferences and workshops which develop the art at the same time they train more people in the necessary primordial understandings of celebration. Groups of lay people in local churches can then get in on the act and joy of enabling vital worship in their churches and communities. For too long worship has been the exclusive possession of people long dead—or of a pastor who all by himself tinkers away at it. Communal celebration—rightly originated—opens the door to the exercise of the priesthood of all concerned believers who are willing to undergo the rigors necessary to do the job well and authentically. I have here tried to set down some fundamental theory out of which many inventions can be made and many people take leadership in the celebrative life.

I too am scared that training in founding ideas and languages and design may make celebration wooden. But it need not. Rather it could be liberating of our true creativity. The opposite is formless chaos and well-meant inadequacy so that

8

the whole enterprise of celebration becomes distasteful through malpractice.

Even greater spontaneity—and courage for freshness— comes when we possess at a *preconscious level* (in our nerves and muscles and patterns of synapses) the resources necessary to do something. Then we do not need to stop or worry because we can't do what the up-bubbling within us calls us to do. Or in dis-ease observe "there's a lot here that we're about to lose forever because we can't capture it and put it into significant form." We must keep celebration as expressive spontaneity, but we do that by being a good friend of it and enabling it.

I use the adjective "contemporary" in the title of this book. Why?

Because new modes of communal celebration are emerging. Not that the old ones were bad, but that ever so often a generation must say things in new ways, with new languages, new forms . . . else the vital impulse of man dies aborning— smothered by the once good which now would substitute its product for the living process.

"Contemporary" also means "simultaneous with living." Don't wait until all is safely dead to celebrate. Such as a church awaiting its hundredth anniversary to celebrate its distinctive life—all the ways of confining celebration to victories long past, rather than doing it in the *midst* of present struggle and exaltation. We can enjoy and glorify now.

"Contemporary" also suggests "contemporaneous." Contemporaneous with the men and women, young people, boys and girls, news events that compose *our life world.* Cease ignoring their existence, their cry, their overpowering desire for relationship. Gather them together in celebration, and member them.

In religious discourse this word "contemporary" also means to live contemporaneous now with the living Christ, of whom

9

it has been said "only in the midst of the world is Christ, Christ."

Contemporary celebration roots itself in lived moments. We are not celebrating cloud nine or our own emotions, or how sensational we feel when we "let go." We are celebrating a reality which we find at work in our world at particular points in very concrete encounters. We are transforming epochal events into meanings and the culture of a people.

Many celebrations are—and will be—surfacy. But more and more the deeps within ourselves and the folds of life can reveal their fascination and tremendous power and the peace of the quickened seed will become our peace.

Partly as an aid to such, I have put what I call an "exploration" after the logical presentation of each chapter. These explorations are a paralogical way of grasping the forming real in poetic rather than propositional forms. I hope the transitions to them will not be too jarring, but enough so that they open up new options.

# Contents

THE TIME
OF CELEBRATION
IS AT HAND

# 1.

# Possible and Needful

Life is so full of tensions, problems, possibilities developing, that we must *find peace in becoming and within struggle.*

Unless a person finds his founding relationship and his center—and joys in them—his own life on earth is but a succession of sound and fury, programmed sensations. crises, diffuse spending in all directions. Until he as person is spent—sometimes never even gets born.

We live in a precarious and permanently ambiguous world. There is no assurance that mankind will not destroy mankind.

But in the meantime we must *live* our lives. *We* must live our lives.

We can choose to see ourselves as victims of society and kept patients of a civilization that is a vast mental hospital. Or we can live in enjoyment and celebration of the bit of good that is in the lived moments granted to us, and in the people we meet.

Our peace will be a "nevertheless"—a making of all things

15

freshly new each morning, an offering of new creation to fellowman (which they may or may not accept), a living toward possibility and a Promised Land even as we dwell in a wilderness. The only peace we can know is tension transformed by commitment.

We have enough people who have lost their nerve. Enough "forever sucklings" trying to substitute the externalities of an affluent society for food of the soul. Enough mass communication reeking with porno-violence, and proud that it is. Enough people all over the world whose lives are burning resentments, vociferous hatred, fear of other people. We have enough rootless, normless, sanctionless, planless people incapable of family life and of history-making. Enough novelists, poets, writers of movie plots and TV shows whose stock in trade is sick, sick, sick.

> Invalids
> using a language full of woefulness
> to tell us where it hurts, instead of sternly
> transmuting into words those selves of theirs,
> as cathedral carvers
> transposed themselves into the constant stone.[1]

Already we have too many tepid church members and eleven o'clock sacred assemblies that have gone limp and numb. Within the pastorate and official boards we already have too many moaners, and groaners, "aginers," impotents, people-rejecting "prophets." Already surprise, wonder, awe, tremendous and fascinating mystery, the outbreaking of the Holy Spirit within a congregation, are but feeble memories of great-grandfather's days or of the new-born Christians twenty centuries removed.

Further, just in order to survive today, a person must make an affirmation. And develop it with some others.

[1] Rainer Maria Rilke, "Requiem," *Selected poems* (Baltimore: Penguin Books, 1964), p. 58. Used by permission.

## CONSUMMATION AND DELIGHT—NOT MERELY SOLVING PROBLEMS

Human life is more than trying to solve problems, learn how to use the world, fight the onrush of grim necessities. A human being has a right to enjoyment. Moments when the flower of experience flames in wonderful completion.

The Calvinists—together with a high sense of vocation—put in their Catechism:

"What is the chief end of man?

The chief end of man is to glorify God and enjoy him forever."

We were meant to enjoy, to delight, to celebrate. To be fascinated by Presence, Mystery. To be wonder, amazement, surge of realization. To be so sensitive to patterns of beauty that they instress us and dwell in us from that time on.

To be fully human is to have consummatory experience— when many lengths of experiences come into conjunction, and the worth of them hits us all at once. Instead of continuing to rush about, we take in, appreciate, we sense what it all means. We feel the flowing generosity of communion and consummation. The altogether lovely is present, not merely longed-for. We cleave to that which is good, until we become one body with it.

There are evils in the world which must be fought and problems which must be worked on. And they must not be ignored. But if our attention is constantly only upon them (or if this is all church is about), we become eroded, rigid, drained of warmth, dehumanized.

For we *become* what captures our attention. What we put as the focus, rather than the fringes of our attention, determines our habitual center of personal energies.

We choose the *focus* of our attention as we journey through life . . .

17

Upon darkness
   or upon a clearing of light?
Upon the evil in the world
   or upon saving truth?
Upon problems
   or possibility?
Upon polluting ugliness
   or upon beauty inviting our participation?

It is not merely that man needs a change from constant battle. Though he does need periods of "Sabbath rest" when, instead of continuous flying into headwinds, he perches on a tree by the rivers of water, intakes beauty, sings his song honoring the sunrise and his territory.

The essential question is—what is his predominant tuning even while fighting and solving problems?

Is it predominantly celebrative . . . or despondent, numb, dominating? Condemnatory . . . or, as with Dietrich Bonhoeffer, thankfulness for being vividly caught up in his people's fateful travail—horrible as it was?

Today we hunger to live out of perfected joy . . . which no event can rob us of.


## ALONENESS IN A WORLD OF DISAPPEARANCES

In some of his moments of awareness—man is ghastly aloneness in a world of disappearances.

To be entertained is not enough. To delight in is not enough. To be a functioning part of an organization is not enough. To find friends in a coming and going institution is not enough.

Man wonders if there is any fundamental belonging and good earth which will not be taken away from him . . . or if he has founded his life on sands over which the caravan of life passes only into a shadow.

18

Are there goings-on of continuing creation with which he can keep in touch? Is he part of something which an intelligent and knowledgeable man can affirm? Within which he can have being rather than nothingness? Is he moving with the fundamental rhythms?

A *human* being seeks at-one-ing with the Innermost Moving. Religious-ontological loneliness is unbearable. Life in unfathomable darkness, visited occasionally by sensations darting and passing-meteor showers of event, is frightening.

And when he is himself, man is not only a hunger for belonging and founding. He belongs as an *understanding* potentiality-for-being. Life without huts of meaning—in which he gathers round a hearthfire and a table with fellowman—is struggle against ceaselessly windswept desolation.

And as we observe the closed minds and closed fists men raise today as their symbols *forward,* we feel the need for occasions, relationships, languages, which untighten, unfreeze, relocate contemporary man. Homeostasis—the tendency of all organisms to return to the same form and level of energy pattern—is both a health and a sin in man. Future is possible only if new inputs occur and man leaps into a new level of exciting possibility. Sometimes he must be moved on from where and what he now is, by a tide whose advancing line cannot be stopped.

## PURELY INDIVIDUAL EXISTENCE IS NOT ENOUGH
## THE EMERGENCE OF PEOPLENESS

Contemporary communal celebration is arising also because we all feel that merely individual existence is not enough. We must together form A People, create together a symbol system which gives us meaningful world. Life outside some intersubjectivity is too frightening, too precarious for everybody. We cannot even be human!

The rush all over the earth to get into some tribalism is an expression of man's acute hunger to belong to a system of present power and relationship, an available supply of sanctiond meanings, a thrust moving against much of the times toward a destiny. In other words, to belong to a People.

Vigorous men are aware that we are no longer peasants, but persons. And we are all lost, unless large numbers of such people begin to *participate in making some kind of common humanity.* Unless they join in acts of creation and redemption that will constitute *life* world in the places where they are located.

These contemporary pressures and goings-on toward peopleness—felt with great intensity—develop enterprises of communal celebration. Where and when—and in whatever sizes —this thrust toward peopleness is realizing itself, communal celebration will be significant part of its growing. Effective leaders of new life will be especially skilled in enabling celebration—whether their People is a team of persons working on a cause, a group of college students, a school, a staff of an institution, a family, a world youth culture, a movement of man toward humanity. The scope and service of communal arting and religious celebration burgeons in all directions.

For today's man is out to find a troth . . . something that is true to him, and to which he is true. A fidelity from which all kinds of choosings and consequences follow.

He must help architect a culture, jointly create with others meanings which give him intelligence and spine to stand up.

## CREATING AND ARTING BY THE MILLIONS

We now have mass art for, by, and of the millions.

The whole population is not only demanding aesthetic quality in the products they buy, but creating their own art.

The very existence of television has popularized making out

with a guitar, forming a band combo, composing your own songs and lyrics, making your own tapes, experimenting with sounds and lights and colors.

We now have not so much the lone balladeer as "singing guitars" all over the place. Not so much the listener to music as the composer of music and writer of lyrics that express "I am the man, this is what happened to me, this goes on inside me." Not the withdrawn painter brushing into form the hallowed past (or his viscera), but the citizen using all kinds of media to express significantly what is going on now—and as it appears to him. We have an onrush of new folk arts. Everybody is taking the photos they want to make, instead of calling in the community expert. And this now spreads to making their own 8mm short movie—not just of a trip they took, but of a plot they want to present as an understanding of life. "I will be heard, I will appear."

What has been called the lumpenproletariat is rapidly disappearing. Or, if you prefer, it is asserting its own folk art. And the style and message becomes worldwide.

Among us is a vast stirring into expressive life. Hopefully that is also an awakening of each person's possibility for humanness. "Potential" becomes a favorite synonym for man, and the world.

There is a massive move into folk . . . into soul.

Now is the time for the sunrise of imagination, and the enabling disciplines of expressive skills.

TO VOICE THE HUMAN CRIES OF OUR TIMES
TO PROVIDE AN OCCASION WHERE
THEY CAN BE HEARD
TO ENTER INTO THE SIGNIFICANT FUTURE IN THEM

Who ever heard a human cry in a church service?
Until it spiraled against the girders, rattled the windows,

21

upset all air currents, smashed into the sensibilities of all people present and awakened them as never before?

It's about time.

*To voice the human cries of our time;* and *to enter into the significant future that might come through them* could be done in celebrative worship. It is a distinctive mark of *contemporary* celebration to sense and to feel thoroughly as never before; to take into ourselves the human cries that *today* a God who is interfaced with humanity would be hearing.

What cries might be heard and celebrated? What are the originating, terrible, magnificent, *energies-on-the-loose,* now speaking their existence situation?

> The cry of a man for others to be open to him in love. Of our country's divided people—"bring us together."

> Lost in darkness! Losing control! Cut off from the land of the living! The wail of one who no longer wishes to be an impervious, impersonal thing, but a warmly human *subject.* And cannot find the way.

> The stark moral demand that cuts away all excuses, pretense. The cry of a group in our community that has been long violated and again profaned, "You Are the Man!"

> "The world has done me wrong. I object!"

> "The dream mighty of wings" "La causa!" "Sodom and Gomorrah are not our home, but new possibility whose time has come."

> A moment of freedom calling to other freedoms. The roar of rage. The wrath—undigested and uncontrolled.

The cry of a man who has come through. "I am! I did!"

"News! News!"

"The time which on earth is granted me is passing!"

"I who want to be kind, am forced to kill. Formed to create, I spend my life destroying."

"My God, my God, is there nothing to awaken humanity in us, and unite all humanity? Inhumanity is exploding the world."

What future do we see in these cries? Form from them?

## NEW LANGUAGES
## NEW MEANS OF EXPRESSING

These cries can now be put into *languages* which can be made generously available and are understood worldwide. Into languages which are energy at the speed of light and are right now in their *formative* stage. Into languages which put a *total* content of "mind" (feeling, intending, experiencing, visioning, thinking, manufacturing meanings) into one package. Languages that have the presentational immediacy of a painting of Niagara Falls that puts us right at the precipice going over with the water, but also in a sky that locates it in a universe of moreness.

These languages are a new fact. We are to use them in stating the future and forming men.

They are the mass arts often called electronic communications. And we are to mobilize all of them into overwhelming communal communication. And to the person in his private room.

We can no longer restrict ourselves—nor do people intend

23

to restrict themselves—to the constant intrusion of merely verbal abstractions between themselves and reality, between themselves and encounter, between themselves and aliveness.

And gilded worship services cannot birth us. Only Pentecosts in which we receive from the full arc of the world, and from which we send out a news that can be understood in the languages that are understood worldwide. And are generously available.

These languages are also the new modes and dimensions of human consciousness that are upon us. With which we create our moment of mankind, develop this generation of MAN. New "tools" of expressing ourself as man.

*Contemporary* man will learn to read and create these new arts and media. And to mass them in communal celebration.

## EXPLORATION

Each time we complete the logical development of a line of thought in a chapter, we will soar off on one aspect, and develop it in more poetic art form. I call these "explorations." Here is the one for this chapter.

# EXPLORATION

When I wake up
I return from *nowhere nothingness*
into the land of the living

    Once more
      the burning fountain
        flares into consciousness.

    Out of diffusion
      I come into focus
    Out of brooding night
      I come as cloudy sunrise streaked with light

    Out of the encompassing
      whose margins only I touch
        I careen toward eternity.

(2)

When I wake up
  Once more
    I am poetry of the present
      the white seething incandescence of the incarnating
        moment
        "Here in this very instant
        up bubbles the stream of time."

Once more
  I selve a body—
    "I find myself
      Something more highly pitched
      selved

and distinctive
than anything else in the world."

Once more
  I have a name.

(3)

When I wake up
  from sleep's let go

Once more
  I put together worlds
    of life or demonry

Once more
  the things of the world
    are taken into the world of the personal.

Once more
  my troths
    begin to image and to choose

Once more
  I enter
    the creating and impairing of the cosmos
  shouting—or whimpering—
  "Here comes me."

(4)

Once more
Out of shut-up-ness in oblivion

26

I run
for communication and communion

Once more
daylight people
awaken each other
develop together.

Once more
my ascension
into the Society of Transformers.

(5)

When I wake up
I emerge
as person-saturated-with-culture
containing all that I have met and experienced
from whom I got the language,
the connections,
the possibilities of journey,
for my one life on earth.

Out of this culture
I-as-expressive-spontaneity leap
a curve of melody . . . buzzing with noise!

(6)

Once more
time ripens.

A tradition rhythms and journeys forward
  the  momentum
    beat
      tune
        throng of echoing rhyme
        of My People
    moves again through time toward a destiny

Once more I take up a particular place
  in a world net
    of thinking men
      in communication with one another
        each open to becoming more than he now is.

# 11 WHAT IS CELEBRATION?

# 2.

# The Essential Act

What is really going on in celebrative actions? More than meets the eye.

Celebration is living with a certain headlong vitality, sensing immediacy of the Inner Moving of all existence.

To celebrate is to enter the Creating and Transforming which is now making mankind, has made mankind, and will make mankind. In wonder, awe, realization, total participation.

Celebration is entering into what makes possible human existence with such momentum of delight and valuing that we are awakened and enabled to take part in world-forming from the inside.

Celebration is Shalom. For the moment, all things find their true place and promise of completion. The celebrator wakens out of boredom, stupor, mediocrity. He is in and with a world pervaded and held together by tremendous and fascinating mystery. Along with his fellow men, he is incarnating and membered.

Ultimately, therefore, celebration is *corporate*, not individual event.

Little Jack Horner, sitting in a corner, eating his Christmas pie, exclaiming to himself, "What a great boy am I!" is not celebration. Rather it is decadence—the loss of a sense that there is an *otherness* without which we do not exist and which undeniably is whether we want it to be or not. With a loss of this sense all the world is reduced to the irreality of plastic flowers with which we decorate graves—which we have manufactured out of ourselves.

Little Jack Horner made two mistakes—he thought he could celebrate all by himself and in a corner, and he thought he could celebrate himself.

We celebrate not ourselves, but the forces which make the human. "We are the greatest city, the greatest nation, nothing like us ever was" is profane idolatry, not celebration.

Many people also mistakenly feel that celebration is exclusively "HIP! HIP! Hurrah!"

But entering into what is making the human includes living the tragedies of our people and the choosing of suffering for the joy which is set before. Any celebration which does not include these elements sickens and withers for lack of depth.

Celebration is taking into one's consciousness the *full range* of the human condition and in such a way as to sense the human dignity present. Only in such celebration do we discover ourselves, and the hiddenness of God becomes unhidden.

Not "all's right with me and the world," but headlong vitality is the key note of celebration.

Freshness, immediacy, hilaritas, consummation, distinguish the energies of celebration.

## HEADLONG VITALITY AS THE STYLE OF CELEBRATION

Celebrative existence is *expressive*, rather than reactive. We are not trying to solve a problem, but are in process of incarnating a truth.

32

We are not merely an integrity, but an expressive, spontaneous integrity; not merely a being, but a becoming being. So we feel creation moving through us.

Our imagination stirs, a wild exuberance begins to flow. It takes on form, pattern, structure, relationship. Our now undivided energies pour into the shaping of a world of meaning. The invisible within us becoming visible. We are acting—not because we need to defend ourselves or to release glandular tensions, but as Presence appearing to itself. We are *in* our acts and words. Morale rises within us as at last a work is about to be completed, and we sense that it says something of what we want our life to say. Even though it is not perfect, something that is a mixture of God's image and our image has been incorporated into a bit of world. And we feel "I am but one small man, but the cause I serve is tremendous."

This integral headlong vitality is *celebrative* existence.

Such profound functioning has greater vitality in those who know the risks, have endured the insults and are no longer afraid of them, have been to hell and back. The naïve cannot really *celebrate*. They have never acquired all that is necessary for this style of existence. Like Kierkegaard's "admirers" of Christ, the naïve think that celebration consists in shouting "hurrah." They gape and roar at the fireworks others send up to startle and amuse them.

### LIFE STYLE

So first of all celebration is a style of life. It is a synonym for "hilaritas"—a word used for centuries in the Christian community to name a life which is courage enjoying freedom.

Hilaritas is a lively confidence that what one is doing will put forward the world even though the immediate society does not approve. It is doing the relevant thing because the wholeness of ourselves leaps up toward life. But it is not naïve. It comes *after* we are aware of evil and defeat, but still see growth and beauty. After we have endured conflicts and dark moments, but were not overcome by them. Faced with rampant evil in an ambiguous world, we were able to utter "nevertheless."

Hilaritas is Abraham going out, not knowing where he was going; Moses forsaking Egypt, not fearing the wrath of the King; Jesus of Nazareth finding a relationship to God which he clung to in preference to all else, St. Francis, despising all possessions for in-being in love; Bonhoeffer placing himself at a crossroads of conflict where Christ was suffering at the hands of an evil world and taking the consequences in triumph. Hilaritas in our own time was John Kennedy for whose life we might say—and at the same time hope for our own lives—

> "The future is now. I can help it be born
> The rotting past does not have dominion.
> Life is tough and the world is precarious,
> but I live in New Time not Old Time.
> Sometimes courage forms my speaking words—
> and it feels awfully good. I will not
> play the other fellow's game. I've
> discovered a truth I am."

Of such nature is celebration as a style of life.

## COMMUNAL EVENT

Celebration is not only a style of life, but a culturing of experiences with the help of other people.

To some degree this happens *as* the experiencing is going on—and is a large part of the experiencing. Without this simultaneous realization, any later culturing has too much the character of celebrating cloud nine while bound in a hot, eroded desert.

But not all is simultaneous. There are also later times when the experience is re-lived, re-seen, re-valued, put into such compelling form that it becomes more than we first knew it to be. It develops, fills out, co-creates with intersubjectivity, becomes more widely possessed by the corporate group with which our life is intertwined. Celebration is communal event.

In celebration A People receives news concerning victories, defeats, crisis points. It repossesses and recenters its originating coming into being. Reasserts in significant symbol its deepest feelings and troth (a choice from which all other choices flow), rehearses distinctive transactions with the world. Consciously affirms its history-making and continues "the next spiral around the mountain."

Communal celebration is "A People" clarifying, intensifying, putting into significant form their particular mode of hilaritas. And so becoming even more "members one of another." Sufferings and triumphs and celebration have wrapped them all in a single fate. No one is left out. They have an enterprise moving through time toward a destiny. There is a song to be sung, a journey to be made, a territory to be colonized.

## A STORY

A Celebration therefore must not be thought of as a "program to be put on," but as a length of development, culminating in community meeting.

1. It begins with "A People." Persons who become members one of another and have an enterprise.
2. Individuals, a team, the total group, have vivid experience. Preferably cumulative experiencings over a period of time.
   News comes of related events.
3. The experience and news are "arted" into meanings and

35

image of the life world. (There is a transcendence of *actuality*. It becomes more than it was.)

4. Communal celebration is designed. A community gathers, treasures, creates.

The meanings become corporate culture—preferably expressed multi-dimensionally. The People moves into new experience.

Expanded into a somewhat dramatic form, the developing sequence can be stated as follows—

## Scene 1. *A People*

The ground of all celebration
  is a circle of people
    who believe in one another
      and in something together.

## Scene 2. *Live an Encounter*

Who have recently
  had a lived moment
    that stirred in them
      pulsing significance
        that now cries out
          to be explored and articulated

They are a windswept ocean
  of feeling and valuing
    surging vitality

Multiple strategies swirl through them
  of tuning into or out, moving with or against
    evading, consuming, exploiting,
      delighting in.

Scene 3. *Search into It to Find What Is There*

They enter
the lived moment
look around in it

Re-live it in a fresh way
"I am the person. I was there
This was my existence situation"

Discover the
"for sake of which" . . . the concern
the intentional arc
which formed this bit of world

They name this life world
the forces that are constructing it
how significant they are

Uncover the wealth in this lived space
so they may know where to place themselves
the next time.

Scene 4. *Sense Potential and Vision Future*

But they do not stay frozen in the experience
They are instressed with beauty!
possible world opens out.
potential begins to rush pell-mell
existence-for-them starts developing

They say a fascinated "yes"
to one of the burgeoning futures

They say
"Nevertheless" to counter pressures
"No" to rottenness

They put together a future-past-present

that gives new time
and morale

An ecology of meanings
in which they can dwell together
and create mankind in humanness

They go with expectancy. Sensing—
Horizon
Transcendence
The transhistorical

## CONSUMMATORY

Celebration is consummatory experience. The whole sum of many digits (details, events) is present. Completed—in the sense that the enjoyment which belongs to the outcome of our enterprise is present right now. As—for instance—the satisfactions of harvesting and of being a part of the growing enterprise of the whole world can be present in the moment when the farmer is sowing the seed.

The satisfaction, the significance, the burst of delight which belongs to the finalities of life, fill the present moment. A filled present exists us. The end outcome—and our joy in it—are present in the moment of partial achievement. Even though we know that we will never achieve its full realization in the objective world, the beauty of the whole instresses us, and we are at peace with it.

But we do have some sense of workmanship about it. And strongly feel that we are not celebrating an ideal, but have enjoyment grounded in actual experience. This happened—and to us!

The meaning of the whole enterprise *touches what we are doing*—and our world (both inner and outer) lights up. The glory shines through and round about. Epiphany!

38

## EXPLORATION I

He Who Wonders met Celebrators. And he asked them—
"Why are you coming together?"
  And they said—"That we may enter the Coming Kingdom,
  which is even now at hand."

You sound as though you really expect something to happen.
  Yes. Our first action together is to celebrate the glorious
  liberty of the sons of God.

What do you mean by "celebrate"?
  By "celebrate" we mean—"to appropriate into ourselves,
  with reverence and enthusiasm, the life which has made and
  is making us a people."

Just what is this "glorious liberty of the sons of God"?—More
than just a pious phrase?
  We celebrate the God out of which new personal life comes.
  Because there is this God, we can be free from what we
  already are, and from uncertain fumbling.

Celebration is freeing?
  We belong to a creating that goes through and beyond our
  group, our provincial community, our membership in a particular race or nation.

This I would like to see.
  Nor are we altogether limited by the here and now. The
  memories and achievements of people of the generations are
  part of the roominess of our lives. And expectancy takes the
  lid off our energies.

Would it not be truer if you said—"We live according to the
teachings of the past—like museum pieces in a living world?"
  We celebrate a God whom man cannot carry around in a
  box, sacred words or laws, saying "Now we've got him."

39

God is always breaking out with new surprises, in unexpected places and events. And this too is our freedom. Both God and man are a spring of life.

This liberty and this God are quite important to you, then! Yes, when we come together in celebration, we let go of our tense awareness of ourselves. So our energies flow.

Isn't your idea of celebration sort of heretical, way-out, fundamentally irreligious? No. Celebration as *entering into* is the Prayer of Humble Access in the classic communion service—"that we may evermore dwell in Him, and He in us." Celebration is what we mean when we say "Celebrate the Lord's Supper."

Therefore, "to celebrate" is a much more accurate, potent, and historic word than "to worship." A "service of worship" seems to be a long-time anachronism.

# EXPLORATION II

Celebration is a million candles lit with reverence and joy.
   Are we then to plod along, unfilled by the galloping intensity
   at the heart of things?

Celebration is a crash of cymbals and a torrent of trumpets
pouring through cracks in the drum roll of death and destruction.
   The rotting past and the disappearing present shall not have
   dominion.

Celebration is intersubjectivity with a man intensely aware of
"to this end was I born to bear witness to the truth."
   And newness of life begins for us.

Celebration is offering the agony and creation of this one day
in the whole world to a transforming God.
   We are transformed by participating in the transforming.

Celebration is the earth seen by an astronaut, stars seen
through a telescope, the beating of heart muscles as seen
with a fluoroscope.
   We see better than we usually do what's really working in
   the world.

Celebration is the sudden rush of meaning when things come
together.
   Jumble and chaos fall into pattern, and we shout "Eureka"!

Celebration is the cascading communication of a circle of people who believe in one another and in something together.
   The sound is deep and loud . . . in languages all mankind
   can understand.

41

Celebration is a people setting out through time toward a destiny.

There's a journey to be made.

A song to be sung.

A narrow pass to be found toward a horizon; time and space to be made fit for human beings.

# III CELEBRATION'S INTERPERSONAL EVENTS

# 3.

# Mode of Relationship

Celebration is a mode of relationship. It is not a spectacle viewed by people who remain impervious to each other.

It is a special kind of relationship which can best be described by words which Gabriel Marcel uses—Presence, Mystery, Encounter, Awakening, Co-nascence.

## PRESENCE

I sense people as Presence when their *person nature* pours out in my direction.

Here is a "to be respected" center . . . that has to be met partly on its terms—not merely something to be had by me. Or something to be consumed.

Here immediately head-on is a depth of powerful consciousness which exists in its own right. Which I can only partly comprehend. I am fascinated with its unpredictable possibility —even in awe of it. It appears as a rather perfect expression of its nature and its integrity. It is not trying to be what it

45

thinks I want it to be, but is actively about being a person. I sense feelings, valuings, comprehendings, going on. This reality is not a flat surface that can be understood by those who rush by, but an inwardness that cares with intensity, intends to have to do with me, is multi-dimensional.

I sense a creator, rather than a *created thing*. This is not another product, but something that means to mean. Here is a *selfed* consciousness.

At this very moment it is intentionality and meaning to have destiny. Something is incarnating here and now . . . which I do not control, but can only lure and influence. Which I dare not profane, nor want to.

So a Presence awakens me as nothing else in the world can do. A personal freedom coming toward me evokes something new out of my depths, tunes me into being creative also.

So important things happen. Simultaneously in the instant when I become aware of other persons as Presence and Mystery, I become aware of myself as Presence, I become present to myself, I become Presence and Mystery.

"With," "in," "for," are the words which symbolize our relationship. When we encounter another as Presence and Mystery, we are not alien or external to one another. We are becoming interior to one another.

Of all the phenomena of the earth, Spirit (a Presence) is most able to enter and be entered into, to be incorporated into another's existence. To create together what is not yet.

However, Spirit, Mystery, Presence is never available in its *entirety*. It is felt as a depth within depths—a revealing that has still more to reveal and to be evoked. We do not understand all that it is—only its present revelation. But enough comes through that we are drawn into further relationship.

Finally—and very importantly—a Presence is something I *believe in*. I believe that this Presence is honestly revealing its multi-layered, multi-dimensional existence. That what I encounter is in fact its expressive spontaneity, its "poetry of the present." I feel that I understand enough of its intent and mode of being-in-the-world that I affirm it as something with which a desirable life world can be built and inhabited together.

We come into being simultaneously—and because of each other. We are mutually freshened. We spring up together as knowing, valuing persons.

Therefore the leadership of a communal celebration cannot be an individual, but must be dyad and dialogic. A *team of freedom and Presence.* And these co-birthing events must be happening in the team, else they cannot happen in the total community.

## INTERSUBJECTIVITY

In this immediacy of the personal is another phenomenon which may be called intersubjectivity.

Intersubjectivity begins when I sense that another will is doing things to the world I want to shape. Not only is my mind putting together what is before me into a picture of a desirable world to live with; other people are doing likewise with the same materials. And the result is not the same.

In this simultaneity, I begin to recognize the existence of another organizer of a self-in-world. He is intentionality—a vortex of dealings with our common environment. He is originating. Often very strong feelings interfuse his actions. He is a *subject,* not just an object which can be pushed around without taking account of this subject nature.

And because of this clash—and in the very frustration of being unable to bring off my world—I become aware very excruciatingly that I too am a subject—an organizer and a thrust to form worlds, and a caring about what happens.

47

This double recognition of subjectness in the other and in myself is the first step to inter-subject existence.

Recognition that each are subject can also come because the other enables my effort. I can experience others as organizers of a momentary life world which enhances, completes, mates with, the little universe of activity I am trying to bring off.

In either frustration or completion, I recognize an *otherness* . . . which is also doing things to the arena that we are shaping up.

If the other is willing, by talking we can discover what the other intends, what vision of possible world-for-me is determining each person's actions. By communication we can begin to see and feel the dynamic feelings regarding the significance of what is happening. If fortunate, we create together a vision and words that enable us to understand the possibility in about the same way. And so can work together within a common climate of feeling in a project we carry out together. We can create something more than either of us alone could have done.

So intersubjectivity is a treasured *field of presence*, illuminated by significant symbol. We are in touch with each other as expressive, valuing centers.

Such intersubjectivity is difficult to bring about in a communal celebration. For it is not the same as arousing common emotions and response to stimuli presented by a leader. It has to be built through actual experiencing of the process. And none of the steps can be left out?

But as it comes off, we begin to move into an intersubjectivity which goes through time. We are on the way to becoming a People.

## PEOPLENESS

In a truly communal celebration, we are not just with-in-for separately understood persons. We also experience *a function-*

*ing organism* of persons. For which "a People" is perhaps the most appropriate name.

A People is a distinctive *structure of life* within which the member places his life. His one life on earth has found its home, its dwelling place, its habitat, the territory where it can now be productive and realize its potential. Such structure of life must be present in celebration.

But "structure" has such a totally impersonal connotation. *Organism of personal life* seems a better term than structure to convey the full meaning. This phrase has more of the necessary tuning, color, warmth, strongly felt cohering. And so is the more exact and concrete term. "Organism" suggests a *functioning system of humanness* in which persons are not only "members one of another," but *together constitute a body*—"bonded and knit together, the whole frame grows through the due activity of each part, and builds itself up." A wholeness, an organismic system, a multiplet of persons endowed with energy is carrying on self-governance and expanding-into-the-world activities. It has identity, and resists attack and destruction.

### Power Field of History-Making

Peopleness is not only organic relationship, but the existence of a *power field* that is able to cause things to happen. This too needs to be present in a celebration.

Perhaps the major characteristic of a People is that it is a sequence of history-making. It has been making history, is able right now to form events, and is also now visioning and creating future. It is newsworthy!

So the heart of being a People is being a *destiny group*. Agents of something marvelously worthwhile whose time has come. In this group's hands lie incarnation or disappearance, success or failure, of this possible new.

49

## Culturing Experience into Significant Symbol

Third, a People is an organism which *cultures* experience, and arrives at intersubjectivity. Contemporary celebration is a treasuring of a community's experience. Intersubjectivity is right there building a universe of sanctioned meaning.

A People is a corporate building of a system of significant symbol—events, persons, words, pictures in the mind which (1) are understood in about the same way, *and they all know that they are,* (2) dependably call out congruent actions in the members, *and they all know they will.* So its members can dwell in this system of significant symbol, and carry on the necessary transaction with the world. Communication and communion within commonly treasured truth is a consummatory delight of being human. For it enables us to become members one of another throughout time.

So that finally, a People is a circle of interlocked arms and interpenetrating minds that *believe in* each other and in something together. A People is a network of experiencing, thinking, believing persons, in honest communication with each other, caring about awakening each other, co-birthing the new—each open to the lure of God to become more than he now is.

Without these functionings of a People and of interpersonal relationships, an attempt to celebrate is merely an agitation of the air.

### EXPLORATION

Two explorations go on from this chapter.

We so often speak of celebration as "informal." What could we possibly mean by that—the absence of artistic excellence and a general jumble? No.

And the heart of the interpersonal is the combination "I-Thou." What *is* the basic event of I-Thou?

# EXPLORATION I

What do we mean by "informal"?
The absence of all "ready-made" things that keep creative
spirit drugged and sleeping
as if a spell were upon the land and the potion had
condemned all to be zombies.
as if all present really are their social front,
social role, accustomed masks.
as if persons present were not interestingly unique.

The absence of all residues and customs that arrogantly,
outrageously, nauseatingly, are always trying to come
between people . . . in order to murder true communication of themselves to each other. And usually have
dominion—particularly in "religious" gatherings. Residues and customs such as . . .

Clothes. Vestments.
Alienated art.
"Symbols" that are not symbols.
Gadgets, games, devices that someone is always trying
to substitute for celebration.
All social engineers.
The cold stare of the impersonal intellect, driven by
the will to power.

By "informal" we mean the presence of

*accessibility to fresh experience*

We are together *within* a situation and an experiencing.
Exploring its thickness . . . and in a multidimensional
way. We are not constricted.

51

The momentum of an attractive expanding pattern that can be entered into . . . is present.

We are experiencing the *forming*, not just the form. The brooding of a dream mighty of wings. Future pulses the present.

Expectancy. "Open the balcony, the hour of the imagination is approaching."

Theologizing, rather than theology.

The outcome is not altogether known. But I am among friends. And could help shape what happens.

Buoyed-up swimming in a depthed lake, with long-known companions. And stars come through the dark.

*Warmth. Flame.*

Verve . . . energies revealing rather than dominating.

Atmosphere that is an invitation to be. *This* universe is creation!

Textures like the flowering fields
and predawn followed by sunrise.

The language we speak instead of the language we write. The *speaking* words of people who are contemporaries.

Subjects. A freedom addressing and awakening other freedoms. And being awakened.

Transported into the interior of an otherness.

Tuned in to what is more than all our verbalizations about it.

A one Humanity suddenly flashes across.

Pentecost.

## EXPLORATION II

(To be sung by two voices)

I cry out
   with a fullness my throat can hardly stand
Far away another cry moves toward me
Corresponding to mine, answering its tones

   I cry out
      with a fullness my throat can hardly stand
   "You are present to me
   You are a free and mighty world which no one can
   compel"

I cry out
   with a fullness my throat can hardly stand
      "No matter how hard pressed you are
      In the darkness there waits an answering cry." [1]

[1] Arranged from Martin Buber.

IV  CELEBRATION
AS FORMING
CULTURE

# 4.

# "Minding"
# Our Experiences
# and the World

Celebration is a communal art. And it is one mode of creating a culture within which we live.

So while the spirit of celebration is spontaneity and the bubbling up of significance feelings, those who design and lead communal celebrations need to be aware of how the human consciousness is working—how it extracts and shapes celebrative existence out of events.

All celebration is engaged in culturing. Naturally and spontaneously we are constantly changing events and experiences into symbols of possible future existence. Some of which we treasure and intensify: some possible futures we despise and try to avoid. The "mind" is always working meanings out of what happens. Presumably the more fullness it sees and understands, the more ample the celebration.

This processing of experiences and event has to go on in the celebration. In fact it is much of the celebration. Otherwise we are trying to celebrate without fresh significance feelings and freshly created meanings.

So we now turn to get the understandings needed by the creators and leaders of celebration. What could they profitably know about how "minding" goes on? How culturing takes place?

First of all as to what "minding" is.

## CONSTITUTING CONSCIOUSNESS

Meaningful world, culture, significant symbol, are all possible because man is a constituting consciousness.

Every human being is trying to make his way into and through the maze of this earth's energies . . . in such a way as to realize himself and the enterprises he cares for.

He is forever organizing a little world for the time being, in which he feels this could be done. He is always "minding" for himself a momentary universe that is an arena for action, and a more enduring universe that is his location of home.

Minding therefore is valuing-seeing-organizing a possible world—which becomes a focused intention to bring this perceived world off *and* mobilize a self that could live it. It is a crucial action throughout a powerful celebration.

We must not think of mind as purely intellectual and problem-solving—it is largely perceptual and feeling capacity. Nor as only the "conscious" aspects of our awareness—it is largely preconscious. Nor as merely its verbal functionings—most productive minding is imaginative forming of new world to live the next instant.

Consciousness therefore is not merely receiving—but tasting, selecting, judging, forming strategies of relationship, re-synthesizing, constituting both self and world.

58

This selecting out and totalizing a meaningful world is driven by two simultaneous activities—

1) a person's driving thrust to form a place and structure to dwell in. To find a multiplet of energies which he can enter, become part of, help form. And so escape the death-bringing suffocation of space that is empty and formless, where there is no otherness to meet, nothing actual with which to co-create a world, no common humanity which communes, no space that can become organism, no home, no time.

2) the drive of all potential that is on the move to bring to some completion its burgeoning becoming. And of a person to become manifest to himself, experience himself as feeling-seeing-thinking-choosing-forming subject.

These two thrusts are the motor of constituting consciousness. The forming-feeling-seeing which they do is the major carrier of celebration.

Celebration freshens, invigorates, restores to wholeness such a consciousness. Takes it on a journey of surprises through country new and old. In celebration, we are especially constituting consciousness.

Therefore a fundamental intent in designing, improvising, participating in, a group celebration is to awaken constituting consciousness and send it careening on a developmental journey toward horizon. *Fundamental* minding must be going on—swirling, spiraling, flaming, architecting.


## FORMING COMMUNAL CULTURE

Having a beginning comprehension of "minding," we can investigate the nature of communal culture.

A culture is a system of perceptions of what is, interfused with the meanings we manufacture. This system of perceivings and meanings is held by a societal group, not merely one individual.

Man lives humanly only within a cultured world. (He no longer does anything merely "naturally.") Only by a culture can a People exist itself as a self-conscious body, and enjoy its being. Man is forever busy creating, consuming culture. He is always immersed in and participating in a culture. Always about transforming his momentum and life space into a multiversity of culture forms.

We cannot understand man—nor help him develop—without understanding the forming of communal culture.

To summarize so far—so that we may highlight this intent of communal celebration—(1) a culture is of, by, for a *people*, not just an individual (2) it is a *system* . . . of meanings and perceptions. (Adhesion to *one* over-learned experience, imprisonment within a cliché, conditioning by those in power, is living as an *arrested culture* barbarian.)

## A CULTURE IS AN ECOLOGY OF
## PERCEIVINGS-MEANINGS

A culture is therefore an ecology of meanings. A whole universe of interacting symbols which present seeings and valuings of the world. And modes of being human.

Some meanings (and their matrix of experiences) are more potent and central than others. But all have their place, function, and time of special importance.

But to say that a culture is an organic system is not to assert that all is harmonious, homogenized, monochrome in color and excitement. An alive culture has contrapuntal melodies, pervasive quality, fundamental thrust and tuning. Just like the ecology of the world of nature, a culture is a *patterning* of vital thrusts, formed by energies on the make. So is an alive celebration.

60

## CULTURE IS HABITAT

Vital culture is always felt as *"my* territory."

Not that one alone possesses it, but that it is filled with "meanings I have experienced, my trails through lived space and time, my enterprises." It is tuned with intense feeling that "I too sing. I have lived this culture, made contribution to it, repeatedly risked action as part of it. And delight that I do."

There is great difference between knowing a culture intellectually-academically, and also knowing it participatively. Between knowing a culture as "those people's culture," and knowing it as the culture which *gives me life and death.* The latter is habitat, the former an interesting bit of information.

"My" culture is a dwelling place where I can live with other people. It is a home. In interaction with it, I have become. Here I find a circle of people who believe in something together—and in one another. And so I know that I am not alien to the human. Here I live as part of a developing organism of meaning, which will receive and set forward whatever meanings I achieve.

By birth, geography, work, we are all *thrown into* some enveloping culture. But this alone is not enough. We do not have habitat until we have willingly taken up a functioning part in it.

And only as some culture becomes a person's habitat, is it possible for him to celebrate.

## MAN CREATES AND USES SYMBOLS
## AND SYMBOL SYSTEMS

We come back then to the wonderful power of human consciousness to create and use symbols. For without symbols, there is no capacity to create and cumulate culture. Culture and culturing are possible because human consciousness transforms experiences and meanings into symbols.

This transformation is part of man's nuclear power to constitute "worlds." He presents to himself his preconscious perceptions and proto-meanings by the use of symbols. He also organizes a symbol system with which he can arrange present world into more desirable world.

Which symbols he uses to interpret what an event means to him, what supply of symbols he has available with which to perceive and think, his skill in arranging beautiful and burgeoning patterns of symbols—makes difference in the world.

But he must keep clear that the symbol system is not the existential meaning nor the actual otherness of the world. The system of symbols only enables them to be objectified, freed from bondage to the moment, and presented to his judging and governance center. And to be shared with other people at many times and places. But the existential meaning is always *what is happening in the constituting consciousness* of the particular person at the moment it is happening. A disconnected *"verbal counter"* is *not a symbol.*

Therefore celebration must get back to the original experience of existence which the symbols symbolize. And offer opportunity for multi-form ways of symbolizing. The meaning can then become grown-up and lively, and find membership in a system of meanings.

We must hunger and thirst for the *accurate* word for a situation and for the state of our stirred-up consciousness. We must search to find the most competent symbol that will highlight the forming depth of the lived moment that is powerfully energetic in us. Such a symbol moves us toward personal-social healthfulness. Using the "exactly right" symbol is like the joyful experience of putting on the right pair of glasses— the world which was blurred chaos becomes solid form with

62

definite contours against a background. And one can now move freely.

We live in a century with an excruciating history of having the opposite done to us. Where someone is constantly—through advertising, propaganda, group coercion—trying to get us to use words and images of experience that are sickeningly false to the situation we are in.

On the rightful image! To the symbol that will awaken and preserve the powers of *our* consciousness.

## SIGNIFICANT SYMBOL

The emergence of significant symbol which "peoples" those present, is a major achievement of communal celebration.

Significant symbol is the maker of mind and community.

Significant symbol is an event, person, sound, movement, image, word which (1) is understood by a group of persons in about the same way, and *they all know that they do* (2) dependably calls forth congruent actions from these people, and *they all know that it does*.

So celebration and group action in the world are inseparably intertwined. Without both there can never be *significant* symbol—for the celebrating group would have no evidence that the "symbol" does touch the meaning and action system of its members.

By vividly presenting experiences and events, by accurately symbolizing and richly culturing them, by interweaving the meanings of a number of persons, and by the *distinctive addition of delight and fascination,* communal celebration makes possible powerful emergence of significant symbol.

# EXPLORATION

I am not *in* the world as milk is in a container.
  The "in" is different

I refuse to let my life be reduced to external conditions working me over.
  I refuse to let any group harness me into a giant conditioning machine, and reduce me to regurgitating empty phrases and boring actions when the handle is pulled.

I will not be overcome by *external* time
  flooded along
    helplessly
      hopelessly
        numbly
          obediently
            softly
              squashingly.
I intend to be aware the first time round

## (2)

I refuse to be jailed
  within the stockade of my own individual life
    the enclosure of any one event.

I am engaged in a building job
  on the fundamental notions of civilization
    which can light up and organize habitat for me and my people.

## (3)

So I phenomenologize

And the promise of the future

64

that's embedded in the present lived moment
    comes out
So that I see "the energies that are making the tree"

The flying jet which most of the time was obscured by cloud
    is out in clear sky and visible
        Something is revealing itself to me.
A world begins to take on form
    Out of the givens, the intentional arc of my selfed body
        Puts together meaningful world—available—to me.

I become able to understandingly *stand in*
    this particular bit of world

No longer outside;
    an alien looking through a window

I am within it—
    walking around, observing, participating.

I focus in on a fascinating pattern of energy
    until its shape of beauty indwells me
        enters me
            forms a cluster of energy within me.

In a fresh way I can be architect of life
    for I have more to design and build with.
        I begin to see
            everyday

Feelings of significance have been rescued
    from the blizzard of event
        Events are transformed
            into insights

I have fun using words and art
The week has peaks as well as lowlands.

# 5.

# Organs of Meaning
# in Which Consciousness
# and Culture Are Organized

We turn then to examine the important organs of meaning into which we mind the world that we experience. They may also be thought of as forms in which consciousness and culture are organized—fundamental parts of any full-orbed communal celebration.

The present popularization of the concept of ecology impresses in our minds that everything important is a *system,* not just a pile of parts from which we choose and take and safely ignore the rest.

Man lives in an ecology of culture, just as truly as he lives in an ecology of organic universe. Gestalting is a fundamental process within all the world.

To design and hold communal celebrations is to be forming a total ecology of meanings which is the habitat for this people. Not only is man a multi-consciousness. He is a multi-structured culture. A rich *system* of meanings.

What are some of the interacting parts of a full-orbed system of meanings? In what various ways are the tunings, textures, thrusts, meanings of life "packaged"?

If we have some understanding of the fundamental parts of any ecology of meanings, we will know possible components of any communal celebration. And we will respect this gestalting function of the minds of the people participating. The flow and design of a celebration will enable the process to happen also, not just present them a pattern we have formed.

I believe we can identify the following fundamentals in any culture system:

I. Perception of life world in which they are existing themselves.
II. Preferred great ways of being in the world.
III. Expected story of their one life on earth.
IV. The future-past present of a People's enterprise moving through time toward a destiny.
V. The new that is struggling to be born in this moment of history-making. The group that is to bring it off.
VI. The central myth by which creating's plot is made clear and memorable.
VII. Image of desirable person. Model of what it means to exist.

### (1) HERE AND NOW LIFE WORLD

The first product of constituting consciousness is a seeing-feeling of life world. In which and with which we have to exist ourselves.

These lived moments of "here and now life world"—as contrasted with a rehearsal of the long ago past—are the originative beginning of celebration. Celebration begins with this

67

instant of life world, moves through the interweaving of our perceptions of it, into our formulating of the liturgy (the fundamental game) present within this particular event of life world.

Life world is a world of life-death encounter, not a fixed stage setting.

> "this has to do with us. We are in a live volcano, not a dead or neutral one. Out of all that is going on in the universe, *this* complex of energies!
>
> We are in destiny space, and meaningful time.
>
> These are our experiences, this our existence situation and common fate."

This existential quality is the first essential of any life world. Of a person, or of a group.

But each life world also has its specific contents. Since that content varies with the person and time, the structure of a here and now life world has to be freshly stated as answers to questions:

1. What especially vital energies (including our own) are organizing this particular bit of world?
   What attractions and repulsions do these energies have for us? The becoming that is coming off?
2. Where are we in the total pattern?
3. The growing we're trying to do? The project of our life at this moment?
4. What potential and future are actually present here? The paths, obstacles, accelerators to goal?
5. What are our strategies of encountering, tuning in, relating, bringing off the next desirable future out of this life world?

A celebration with impact sets forth the life world of the people present and situates them in it.

## Interweaving Life Worlds: Formulating the Liturgy Present

A culture and a society begin to form when a group of persons—distinguishing and recognizing the workings that are going on in their life world—begin to interweave a common one.

This interweaving and recognition of "life world" liturgy are important functions of communal celebration.

Preferably this interweaving and cocreating is done in a face-to-face situation where mind plays upon mind in such dialogic and dialectic manner that a livable world is created greater than anyone started with. Each feels that it is true to his experiencings, for something of him is in it. Further it is a world in which others will be living with him. And they all understand it in about the same way—and know that they all do.

Today the reporting, interweaving, interpreting, come in huge quantities to us via mass communications. So much so that probably the reporters, commentators, journalists, pop singers are the liturgists for contemporary man.

In the easy-to-feel forms of drama and singing, they present confidently their espoused life worlds. Events regarded as newsworthy from all over the world are packaged so that each day we live simultaneous with history-making (life world for all of us).

We can distinguish two liturgies constantly going on in our world—a profane and a "sacred" liturgy. Celebration of these two liturgies—in secular language—is constantly going on as people tune in to the "media."

69

The liturgy of profane man might be named by such phrases as:

Man was wolf to man

Good people kept their mouths shut, their minds shut, their hands shut

Stupidity once more destroyed the possible

Arrogance had dominion

Resentment burned

Violence wandered the streets in kaleidoscopic pattern

The big lie pollutes the sky.

The Christ liturgy might be identified by such phrases as:

Walls fell down

Differences dialogued; power was shared

People became members one of another

Wisdom was at the crossroads, and there was light

Let justice roll down as waters and righteousness as a mighty stream.

Originality made a gift of future

A person chose to bear more than his share of suffering.

Thus we might begin to present to ourselves the workings going on in our life worlds. And so know better what they really are. And celebrate what gives us significant form.

## (2) PARADIGM EXPERIENCES
## GREAT WAYS OF BEING-IN-THE WORLD

Man organizes life worlds over a period of time. So that each society finally has preferred ways of being-in-the world, which it talks about and treasures.

These may be called paradigm life worlds. Styles of life

worlds—and ways of bringing them off—which for this People are the actualization again and again of Life.

In such an experience, the meaning of life breaks through—and with such power that it becomes a root experience out of which many occasions of desirable life world develop. The experience becomes then more than just one occasion of *life*. It becomes style—a quality design of lived moment and world. Which is so filled with energies that many other lived moments are formed from it—each having its own special contents appropriate to that occasion.

This paradigm becomes an organizer of life. And so makes possible character and a civilization.

A number of persons struggling through history are involved in an experience of such power and outcome that they sense in it an ultimate existential of the human. There is revealed to them an "isness" within all life. They are caught up in an incarnating of the real—which they celebrate the rest of their lives together. This shape of meaningful world becomes right and normative for them. By it they understand and judge many other experiences—both of their personal life and their society's life.

A paradigm experience, then, is a preferred life world. Of exceptional meaning and presence of Mystery.

The person who testifies—

"Communication is not merely a tool to use in handing on Christianity

Communication is the nature of Christian existence" has a paradigm and can celebrate.

Beyond paradigm patterns of immediate life worlds, man forms another totalizing image—a picture of what kind of *universe* this is. He feels a *"world"* life world. Not only in terms of lived space, but also as extending through time.

With such a life world, any particular event fits into "a

71

world" rather than standing alone and alienated. And so has a somewhat anchored meaning. Cumulative development and stability of identity becomes possible both for the person and the culture. Any event can be understood and handled.

Presentation and interweaving of life worlds, entering into particular people's life world, distinguishing and putting into unforgettable form the profane and the Christ liturgies in contemporary event, building up imagery of meaningful world which hold through a sequence of moments and days and geography—these are primal activities of a celebration. We celebrate not ourselves but the life world we are.

Since a human being is always a self-within-some world, we should never celebrate ourselves. Rather we celebrate some *experienced life world* which we have meaningfully helped to put together and placed ourselves within at some strategic point.

*We affirm that this is life world for ourselves and our people.* It is a mighty oasis within a weary land, a home within a wilderness of wild growth. We delight in it.

So we live with exuberance and anticipatory resoluteness—saved from egocentricity.


## (3) PROBABLE BIOGRAPHY OF OUR ONE LIFE ON EARTH

In culture building, we lengthen the life world of particular moments into a "probable biography of my one life on earth." This is another fundamental fact of any ecology of meanings.

Our minds are constantly putting together a continuing movie of the events of our life. Continually interweaving (1) what is now happening (2) with previous events (3) toward a pattern determined by the future it sees now present as possibility.

Thus constituting consciousness not only organizes a simul-

72

taneous pattern of energies in which it can live as of the moment (life world), but also organizes a *becoming* development, a becoming length of existence which is possible story for this person.

Without this activity, we would not develop character (something we dependably are over a length of time and in many situations), or a destiny (where in the ongoing world, we arrive at realization).

The "expected story of my life" personalizes the events of the world in which we live so that they are no longer "out there" or neutral. They become the stuff of our existence.

A probable story of his life which a person passionately believes in, is used by a person to make sense out of all the details of life. Only then does he see himself as meaning something.

The energy level of every person rises or falls to the degree that he can come up with a desirable story. A person confused and baffled lacks both the identity strength and perceiving ability to put together an expected biography of his life. He can only drag from one happening to another. Without story, his life is meaningless.

For a person is Time. A future-past-present that is emerging, developing, disappearing, re-appearing in new form. And when either of these three time dimensions of himself and his world disappear or become too weak or undesirable, he loses a story. And therefore becomes de-humanized.

Always in any society, there will be held many pictures of probable life biography, but it cannot endure as a society unless these are somewhat congruent, i.e., there is a broad future-past-present within which all see their own biography.

Story-making is a major enterprise of all who hope to influence others, or form them into a People—propagandists, politicians, heads of institutions, teachers, clergy.

73

For in order to get any person or a People to move, two contrasting stories must be presented again and again. (1) If things don't change, this will be the dismal story you and yours will live out; (2) this is a *possible* story that is quite different.

This constructing of two stories can be done in celebration— where it is corporately created rather than imprinted and where it is subject to correction and is continually growing.

Always there exists a *probable story* (what it will be if things continue as they now are) a *possible story* (what it would be if things change) and a story that arouses *expectancy*. It is the latter which awakens and empowers our energies. For expectancy has two dimensions—we believe that this story of my life on earth (1) is desirable, and (2) *it will happen.*

To the *expectant,* even more than to the hopeful, belongs the future. The expectant and the hopeful are different from the fantasy-obsessed, though all three are workings of man's imaginative visioning. The hopeful trust something which they believe will form the quality of their future, the expectant believe they see it in motion. The fantasy-obsessed have narrowed down their world to their own internals.

### (4) THE MOVING STORY OF
### "MY PEOPLE"
### THEIR EXPECTED FUTURE-PAST-PRESENT

We all reach about for "my kind of people." The kind with whom we can relax, feel at home, drop down our tense defenses, tune in to harmonious chords, with their help secure the good life.

The basic unit of humanness is a circle of people who believe in one another and in something together.

This circle of people is of various sizes—two, five, an institution, a worldwide historic enterprise. When we find (or realize afresh) any of these sizes of corporateness, we celebrate.

The person who is merely "doing his own thing" finally begins to consume himself in the fires of resentment. The "culture of poverty" is distinguished by its mistrust of all the institutions and rulers of society in which it is not permitted either to have a stake or to participate in governance. So much so in the large city that people cannot even relate to one another in trust, let alone over a period of time. Many affluent people have also come to this condition—for they no longer believe in themselves nor that their society has a rightness and a future.

We live in a time of great impulse in many people toward detaching and disinheriting themselves, who feel that their major identity must be that of Destroyer, but are also driven by an almost frantic effort to find a tribalism, a new era, a new worldwide people. The temptation within both impulses is to do it by packaging clichés and slogan.

But people live together productively only *in* communication. And out of a stock of images (perceptions *and* intensified feelings) which present to them possible corporate structures of their society, which give plan, purpose, governance, and freedom to carry these out. Image-making of our institutions and corporate life is a great industry—which we must all join.

A society (or People) that can be believed in will be felt by the believer to have these voltages:

A future is present and active . . . imagination stirring possibility.

Power to bring off that future. And the power is presently active, not passive. The seen future will happen.

That future—and the People—has a *rightness* to it. It satisfies our sense of right and wrong.

Together these give us a fresh flood of energy. Desirably

75

then, celebration is of a distinctive *Gestalt* of future-past-present. All three dimensions of time. Without the three, we ultimately demoralize.

Celebrated memories of *past* communal successes and defeats may give an apparent cohesiveness, but cohering melts away if not enformed by this *three-dimensional* futurity which is present *now*. We must celebrate some unique "happening right now" occasion of such filled time if the whole span is to be credible and powerful.

Much of celebration, then, is this time-binding of our people as an enterprise. We not only vision the enterprise, we taste, relish, enjoy it, art it into significant symbol. We have consumatory experience of it.

## (5) IDEOLOGY
### A SENSING OF THE EMERGING FUTURE

In a process world of developmental leaps, regressions, plateaus—and a pace of extremely rapid change—we begin to concentrate on sensing and visioning the future that is about to happen. We may tend to lose out the other time dimensions —but not necessarily. But in all cases the future dimension becomes so crucial that we must especially concentrate on it.

So the emergence, clearing up, intensifying, putting into significant form of an ideology becomes a vivid organizer of almost all celebration. The ethos of our ideology pervades our culture, dominates our choices and feeling tone. It puts together the story of *my people*.

An ideology is a sensing of the new that is struggling to be born in this moment of history-making. Plus the expression of this insight in compellingly strong forms that have great fascination and horizon.

It is not a general statement about history, but an insight

76

into this particular moment. Its major purpose is not merely to understand history, but to change it—to *make* history. It is not something which any merely spectator can ever have, but only a risking passionate participant.

Which is why every ideology also defines the probable group which will bring it off, and their enabling disciplines.

## (6) MYTH

From his encounters with the real, man shapes not only a story for his personal life and a story for his people and their history-making, but a story of LIFE.

The story is a statement of the plot which works itself out in all situations and times, but can be seen in starkest, most powerful form in some particular event. "Plot" might also be thought of as the game that one plays a part in, if his life is to mean anything. It enables us to underscore the secret of how the universe works—of how life (particularly "our people") originated—and now develops its true potential.

Such a story which states the originating plot and game of life is called a myth—the largest possible understanding with which we can live, the most vivid presentation of potential yet to be developed, the game going on which creates human beings in this universe, the basic metaphor of a civilization.

This "longest possible and most encompassing story" helps shape our individual story, and tells us how we are one with our fellow man.

As presented by classic Christianity, the plot of life operating in the vast dimensions of the cosmos—and most particularly in all human beings—could be summarized by the themes of creation, fall, redemption, and the choosing of a Chosen People. The acutal working of this plot is concretely reported in the narrative of the Bible. It is to be understood as operating

77

through all time, since the nature of things was set in the very beginning. "In Adam's fall we sinned all," and one man (Christ) paid the ransom for all mankind so that eternal life was ever more available to all men.

The evolutionary vision was the next large design by which all life could be understood and fruitfully explored. All life is *a becoming*—in a pluralistic, precarious unfinished universe that is self-propelled, intertransacting, inter-governed by events of sensitive grasping and participation in one another combined with destroying those unable to survive in the ecology.

This is the myth celebrated at any meeting of scientists or any paper written by present-day scientists. Many attempts have been made to mate these two fundamental myths. Teilhard de Chardin has offered a notable one for contemporary man in his vision of the present evolving stage of our earth as the emergence of a layer of human beings covering the other layers of the earth—toward the becoming of a worldwide network of thinking men, in honest communication with one another, each open to the lure of God to become more than he now is.

Other basic myths used by contemporary man would include popular Freudianism (the climactic end of all the aeons of existence is a man going to bed with a woman). The myth of Dionysus (that eternal life is received in orgy) also has its return.

The Marxist or Communist myth is the most widespread myth whose believers are sure the basic forces causing anything that happens can be understood with certainty and the course of history governed by its believers.

We live more and more in a world dominated by myths— particularly as we become more educated and affluent. The cohesive core of all celebration is some myth—usually a ren-

78

ovated one or a synthesis of our own particular making. New ones keep emerging, simultaneous with history-making. All too frequently people take a partial one such as the myth of *their* people's making and shut out any consideration of how *human life* originates and conflictful elements transformed into a one life—anytime, anywhere.

Implicitly or explicitly, every celebration is held together and powered by a creation story.

## (7) IMAGE OF PERSON
## AND THE DESIRABLE PERSON

Much of celebration is understanding delight in persons. Even of ourselves and our possibilities. We become fascinated by the human. We celebrate existence.

By entering into other persons' lived moments until we "stand in" them, we begin to build up a picture of human possibility that we delight in as good. By exploring our own experiencings of ourselves, we become a Presence to ourselves. And know that we are not altogether bad—there is something we need not be altogether ashamed of. In spite of their ambiguous mix, human existences are to be celebrated.

So in celebration we interweave our possession of admired figures. Intensify our identifications with powerful and fascinating persons who were able to freely be themselves, and make their way into the structures of society. Many people know and approve of them; they possibly might be gatekeepers of opportunity for us.

These working models of being person we take into our becoming. Persons "who have gone before" in journey—whether our own age or historical. Personally and corporately, we celebrate such persons.

And then—in proper context—we celebrate that image mix-

79

ture which we are. A mixture of our image of our potential (what we could be), of our actuality (what we are), of what we think we will be (expectation), of what we think various other people think we are. And all the gaps and strugglings that go on among these four images. Without some distances between them, we lack energy and distinctions. With too great gaps, we give up and are unable to celebrate.

Celebration images us into desirable person.

## EXPLORATION I

I had been sampling the sky two or three times in the early morning, so that I would get out at the right time to see the beginning glow atop the ridge of mountains. Each time it was fully dark, though with a few large stars showing, so that I knew it would not be a cloudy morning. I should keep on getting up.

At 5:30, I could detect a faint glimmer. It was time to get in motion. As I turned on the light and started to dress, my wife got up. I suggested we better drive over to the A-frame cottage and wake the people there.

When we came out the door of the motel and looked east, the striking and unexpected sight was a thin, thin curve of moon up in the sky, against a lower background of a band of very deep rose along the ridge of the mountains, diffusing off into the still encompassing darkness.

We drove over to the A-frame cottage. I went in and made my presence known to my son's family and asked if they wanted to be wakened to go out to see the sun rise. They said yes. So leaving directions where to come, my wife and I drove back and on up around the hill to our favorite viewing place. The other car arrived immediately after us.

After calling their attention to the unexpected surplus of the moon's presence (the youngest child called it a fingernail moon), the next sensing was of the cold—and even more of our potential coldness if we just stood or sat and waited. So I started walking down the path. Our daughter-in-law took to a large rock, and for some time I had a subterranean feeling that she was getting cold.

The next surge of experience was the sudden making translucent of a few very small clouds just over the niche in the mountain.

81

Then I knew that the sunrise would be worthwhile.

Observing this through the telescopic lens of my camera shut out all the rest of the world and intensified what was happening. I was delighted and pushed down the shutter button. A minute later, this translucent field developed another pattern and lighted color, and I made another picture. As I walked over toward the family, warning came, and I turned and shot the tiny first edge of the sun pushing up behind the mountain ridge. It was rising at high speed.

Turning back to look at the family, it was now grouped in an unforgettable silhouette around the rock—a monument through time to man as family, visioned by a dawn.

### 2.

As I now relive these moments, the word for my prevailing life-world during this half hour is Gerard Manley Hopkins' "instress of inscape."

In all three of the most vivid moments, unusual and fresh patterns of beauty were coming into my nervous system and indwelling it. Selected out of the whole world before me and orbed into a special world by the telescopic lens, only this fresh, beautifully structured inscape existed as my life world.

Residues of these moments of perceiving will indwell me the rest of my life and sometimes pop up to give reassuring flesh and blood to my convictions about the nature of reality for a human being and to my positive feeling about life itself.

Further I have lived, experienced, delighted in; and no one can take this actuality away from my future. Nor can they take away other such moments.

### 3.

Once more I wonder—what is man that he is this kind of experiencing? What is delight? What is beauty?

Beauty occurs when the whirling darting energies within myself and the universe no longer collide, but form a *family* of energies—a multiplet—which steps each member up to the speed of light.

Also there was color in this beauty. What was its function?

Color is evidence that a tuning in to each other has already occurred in these energies.

Beauty, then, is what I am when I participate in all such events.

* * * *

These three peaks of experience this morning suggest to me that I am not alien in this universe. In such lived moments I see evidence that I am in touch with it, so tuned to its exciting nature that it can instress me. This experience and conviction I thrust against moments when I do feel estranged from the whole world.

* * * *

And what is delight? Delight begins with spontaneous receptivity to the poetry of the persent.

I had not planned to see the moon—did not know that I would. But I did not refuse to see its total unexpectedness. I knew there would be a sunrise—but the pattern and color of the actual sunrise was available only as it was happening. Poetry is TIME uncovering itself in the actual.

# EXPLORATION II

"My God! Where am I?"

Consciousness seeps into my mind, but my body will not move, it only throbs pain. Pain, numbing, intense, death-life, walking the picket fence to fall into death or life or . . . ? I am awake to pain only, no movement. To try moving yields only white, burning, consuming pain.

A light is softly up there, and gray haze settles over rows of beds, still bodies, some moaning.

Blood caked on my blanket, my blood. Recovery room? For operation? I grope to remember . . . my legs smashed . . . motorcycle . . . doctor says operate . . . this morning. Are they there, my legs? My form is a pile of blankets and blood.

"Ohh, Jesus Christ Almighty!"

Footsteps clip . . . clip . . . clip near me, then a face over my body, unmoved, stony. A voice: "He's ready, call Henry and Ford."

"Nurse, give me a pain shot for Christ's Sake! Ohh, Jesus!"

No answer but clip . . . clip . . . clip away. I slip into a gray peace, away away . . .

The haze is broken by faces, then one face, tear-strained, worried, Karla's asks, "Are you alright?"

I know that face. Crying, laughing, I say desperately, "I love you. I've never said that to you before, but I mean it specially now. I love you in a special way. I'll not say it again, do you understand?"

## II

I was totally inward turning in these moments, very alone, very afraid, and very drugged. My reactions to people were more basic and uncontrollable than they have ever been. Yet

84

through this selfishness and intense struggle over which I had little control, I felt a need to reach outward and touch someone humanly and to be touched in the same way. Yes, I wanted my comfort needs met, but much, much greater than them was an inner need to be reached and to reach. I wanted to know that moments of anguish would contain meaning in the end, that they would bring me back to a world and to people with whom I would find a meaning.

## III

In a broader sense, I see the moment as speaking to a human need. That need being that even in our most subsistent, most-oriented moments, there must be reasons breathing meaning into suffering, into struggle. As instant or brief as that moment is, it is the crux at which our very lives are transformed from futility into more total reasons, providing a thread through all moments, lending them meaning and hope.

—Tim Downs

# 6.

# How to Transform Lived Moments into Meanings and Culture

If celebration depends upon culturing, then we need to develop dependable method of turning lived moments into communal celebration.

Fortunately some years back, men in many different disciplines began to develop what is now called existential phenomenology. So the beginnings of dependable theory and method are at hand.

Phenomenology began as an attempt to establish a science of the *human* world, in complement to the science concerned with the physical energies of the world. It is art-science of man as will-to-meanings.

By studying subjects—rather than objects—we can begin to comprehend the happenings within a *selfed* consciousness. These happenings are the subjective richness by which we escape boredom, and by which we exist ourselves. So the functioning of a selfed consciousness—whose internal textures are intentionality, aspirations, images of new possibility, feeling, choosing, constructing life worlds and self-in-worlds—is the most profitable of all studies. And, in phenomenology, we study—not in order to control others (as technological mind would), but that we might *realize*.

Only with a phenomenologizing relationship to other people can human community be established, not by force, but by interchange of "stirrings" within consciousness. Without possession of the phenomenological style of being *with* other people, we regress to the biting, piercing, gasping mandible by which to get on in the world.

So we now turn to setting forth phenomenologizing as a method of developing a lived moment into meanings and on into communal vision.

## TRANSFORMING SEEING INTO BEAUTY OF MEANING

A lived moment, an experience, an encounter, an event in which we have been involved, is the originating source of all phenomenologizing and celebration. Something has happened that stirs up energies and vivid meanings in us. Celebrations develop out of these contents.

A communal celebration does not come about by selecting a theme, a slogan, a campaign, and imprinting it on people through the use of multi-media. A clever attempt to arouse people's emotions and impulse is not celebration. An audio-visual explanation of an important idea is not celebration. Celebration is the overflow of experience into exultant existence. Celebration cannot be contrived, but it can be arted!

So those who would richly celebrate need to develop the sensibilities and methods by which they can possess an experience and develop it into intense and beautifully formed

87

meanings. The way Cézanne found himself making a painting is one model of how this may be done.

First of all Cézanne went out to meet nature—he made his picture in *location*.

"A minute in the world's life passes! To paint it in its reality!"

He had visited the art museums and was greatly enlivened by the art of those who for him were the great masters. But he scorned to paint his pictures there, or in a classroom or a studio. He painted *in the presence of* that which he was painting.

Why? Today we would say because exposure "to the things themselves" is the first step in creating a world of beauty.

For Cézanne, a picture was the result of "meditation, brush in hand." He could not begin to paint until he achieved a perception which unified everything, until he grasped the secret organization of this bit of nature. For his creation was not a duplication of what was "out there," but a transformation into the same beauty expressed in a painting. "Nature" was metamorphosed into man's culture. Painting was a bringing out of a particular significant relationship, intensified until it became indestructible. Which at the same time was a realization of the "standing together" which is the true condition of the world.

Cézanne's great passion was to realize. First of all, "to realize" meant so to enter into the scene before him that he sensed, felt, formed an image of, the inner structure and color energies of the scene where he had placed himself.

"We must give the image of what we see."

"Realize" also meant to truly and convincingly put this image into tangible form (a painting), making it stand out in remarkable strength in human consciousness. In this sense, "to realize" meant to transmute the reality of the things of the world into the realm of the personal. To realize meant to bring beauty into existence in such a way as to make it present to us.

We now turn to a much more developed exposition of phenomenological method.

## PHENOMENOLOGICAL METHOD

### Step I—Living the Moment

Phenomenologizing begins in living a situation. Everything depends upon this awakening of consciousness, and the quality of its awareness.

Without encounter with otherness, there can be no phenomenologizing. We cannot be aware without being aware of *something*.

So the first step in realizing is having a lived moment of "stirring up" encounter, sensitive humanity, heightened existence.

But unless we understand that even perception and awareness are acts of a constituting consciousness, we will never understand what is going on. Perceiving is not what we usually think of when we say that we "see."

An act of perception (in contrast to a glance) is an act of forming an immediate life world. It is not just a "seeing something." Perception is connecting ourselves to what is there in front of us, in such a way that the multiplicity becomes a little universe—in which, for the moment, we situate ourselves because it contains "possibility-for-me." In the very act of perception, we select out and organize this immediate possible world.

But even more is happening. We have—for this moment—also organized a *self*-in-world. Not only does a perception organize an arena of action, a *self* is mobilized. A length of a particular kind of being is started.

89

All this forming is going on in a *lived* moment together with awareness of *how* it is going on, and the person's valuing of the result.

Such an understanding of the fullness of a lived moment opens us to a much more interesting and profound life journey than was hitherto possible.

We become an artist of human inwardness. We see and sense—not so much the landscape around us, but the *man-scape* in which we are immersed. Most of our seeing and sensing is of persons—personal vitalities that mean to be, that exult in being, that quiver out at us to transform and energize us. We can enjoy being this perceiver of persons. Enjoy being a mind that can present to itself multi-layered vitalities composed of varied wavelengths of human experiencing—reds, greens, yellows, blues—each vibrating its intensity—but in relational richness forming a multiplet that is more than the sum of its parts. In fact encompasses the family of man.

Celebration begins with *lived* moments. By phenomenologizing them, we transform them into culture.


Step II—Re-live the Peak Moment with Particular Attention to the Places of Vivid Feeling and Flares of Significance

A human being keeps re-living and re-playing a length of significant moment—

"Something appeared to me.
Life world was being formed.
Self-in-world was being formed."

Phenomenology has a methodology of expanding an event or experience into a fullness which can be celebrated.

To begin with, it invites us to get back to the sources. To

present to ourselves the experiencing *as it originally happened* (not as we would now judge or reorder it). To collect the data of this particular length of forming life-world and a self-in-world. To feel again the power of the experiencing and its leadings on. To bring up into conscious awareness the multiplicity, the thickness, the nuances and textures of awareness which contain yet undeveloped secrets. To recall *all* the significant contents of consciousness—feelings, intendings, decidings, pictures and imagery flashing in our mind, ideas with which we tried to structure it all, the time-binding with previous experiences and expectancies about future.

You become a combination of journalist, documentary photographer, artist, psychiatric expert in symbolizing the tangled events and jumbles of feeling. You are trying for a "scientific" description—in the sense of getting at what was there whether you liked it or not, whether or not it fits the story you would like to make of it.

Catch in the net of your awareness the darts of events and the fleetings of consciousness. Be an extra-sensitive film that records the lights and the darks, the good and the evil, the vivid nuances of shimmering color, the most rapid and faint movements. Divest yourself of your prejudices which cause you to see only what is already made up in your mind beforehand. Participate once more in the event from within. For this is something no *thing* can do. Be the sensitive research instrument into experiencing which only a human consciousness can be. And into *this particular* lived moment which *only you* experienced as you did. And just now.

So in your description of the life world you formed and experienced, present yourself two things: (1) the forming energies within the people involved and the actions that took place, (2) the flood of feelings, the constructing of life world

91

that you were ceaselessly doing, the controlling drama that kept forming behind your forehead.

Only *you* can report the second, for only you have immediate contact with what goes on in your consciousness—your feelings, intendings, endurings, as the event developed. This content is uniquely *you*. And this content is where the significance lies hidden, waiting for development into meaning and insight into the nature of the forming real.

And since you are going for new possibility (futures that are present but "not yet"), particularly try to capture and symbolize your feelings and sensings that presently are largely pre-conscious—i.e., of which you are not yet fully conscious, but have a vague intimation "something is here. This contains yet hidden meanings and revelations. Here is richness yet to be possessed and colonized."

Celebration emerges in lived moments excellently described —with the perceptions, the feelings, and the existence situation showing. Spoken as from the inside of the experience, rather than as a spectator who is intellectualizing about it as if it had not touched him at any point. Communicated in a streaming propulsive language, capable of representing becoming.

Step III—Transform the Event into Understandings,
     Meanings, Culture. Name them.

The human mind has an insatiable need to establish "what is this which I am encountering? What is this event which is going on? How am I connected into it?"

It must see pattern, discriminate the qualities of the energies, find appropriate names with which to think and talk about this moment of life world.

Such establishing is the next step in phenomenologizing.

Its directives go somewhat as follows.

1. Concentrate on the *pattern* of the experience.
   Recognize the forming energies that produced this life world. What was the organizing "hot center"? What nucleus of a dramatic story would connect it all together?
2. Name accurately *what kind* of world and self-in-world this lived moment was. The *project* of your one life on earth at this particular moment. The *kind* of experiencing that went on within you.
3. Art what you are now discovering. So that it becomes clearer, is focused and intensified, transformed into striking image and developing story.
   (E.g., verbal statement, story and drama, sound and music, painting and visual composition, movie, T.V., celebrative ritual.)
4. Place these namings and conceptualizings in touch with the symbols and meanings which already exist in your consciousness. Let them influence one another, and bring forth something new through both conflict and co-creation.
5. Is there material and architectonic here with which you construct "a hut of meanings and a field of growth" which would be habitat for your life? And successfully invite others to live within it with you?
6. What does this experience—and your process of interpreting it—reveal about your resources of perceiving people and manufacturing meanings? The kind and quality of consciousness you are?

In this phase of phenomenologizing, we are consciously trying to put a meaningful world together as a whole. So that we have a "tree growing by the rivers of water," instead of a pile of sawdust. To see something whole, we have to see its structure, peremptory accents, the pivotal constancy. We throw out

93

all confusing incidentals, strip down the life world to its working essentials. And even then we have to grasp a partially hidden structuring which is the *form* of a tree.

While looking into the experiencing we had, we keep throwing up in our mind a succession of words and phrases—trying each to see what it brings out in relief. To see if it enables us to organize what has been going on into what best to do next.

The name we finally accept as the best name for this experience is crucial. For the naming determines how we understand and act.

So we should not lightly name a person, or event, or life world. We should take time and exercise considerable artistry and wisdom. The first "nominee" may be too much shaped by the angry, fearful, exhausted mind we brought into the experience. The first naming may pay too much attention to only one aspect of the lived moment (any experience is very complex, it is not just one thing). Or we may have grasped only the easily seen surface rather than the determining energies. Our mind may have been too impoverished. For seeing what was in an experience depends upon a rich supply of possible patterns of experience.

In the course of such experimental fitting of symbols and lived moment, we often recognize a recurring *kind* of meaningful experience that we have had before and probably will have in the future. Life begins to take on some integrity, cumulative meaning, at-homeness, enduring connection with people other than ourselves. For we discover the paradigms by which it is ordered and powered.

So we keep wondering, pondering, questioning, exploring both the experience and the accurate complexity of our symbols—

"I felt that I was 'with' this person." But what *is*

'being with' another person? Leaning on
each other in sentimental weakness?"
"In this experience I felt quite free." But what is
freedom? Who is unfree?

Such clarifying of the meanings of the great symbols and
speaking words of a civilization can be a major achievement
of phenomenologizing.

So phenomenologizing opens up exploration of the fellow
who is doing the perceiving, the organizing of worlds, the
interpreting, the giving of meanings. His lived life once again
steps up and confronts him and he can see *himself* freshly as
for the first time.

What was my way *right here* of tuning into the world?
Of establishing habitat? What do I care about most
—as revealed in this particular event? The project of
my one life on earth, if I let what was already moving
in me finish what it was about.

How name my existence condition?

What is my culture equipment for transforming experiences into meanings-to-live?

What personally wrought truth do I have to offer?

Since phenomenologizing is concerned with finally arriving
at intersubjectivity rather than a mind locked in its own present
supply of experiences and verbalisms, the culmination of phase
two (and of all the phases) is communication until intersubjectivity is created. A talking together which shares the
flashes of insight and beauty until we all understand a situa-
tion-event in about the same way, and *know that we do.*
And that we can count on all of us acting within this meaning when a novel but similar situation comes up. For we have
a disciplined way of minding experiences and events. We have
phenomenological style!

Illustration of the Product of the
Second Phase of Phenomenologizing

The productivity which comes from doing well this second phase of phenomenologizing may be illustrated by Max Scheler's classic statement of the social-personal structure and dynamics of resentment.

Resentment—as Scheler develops his understanding of it— is a very complex *state of being*, not just a momentary condition. Its "essence" (or nuclear structure) is an experience of intensely felt injustice, combined with a feeling of impotence that one dare not and cannot do anything about it. Not even dare communicate it to the person doing the injustice (and who couldn't care less). As a consequence the resenting person keeps going over and over the event, the hurt of the injustice done and the person doing it, his anger at himself for being so weak and empty of courage. Each time the burning flares more and more into a holocaust of destruction.

With such an analysis, we know that resentment is not the same as anger. Knowing something of its becoming story, we can—if we want to—avoid treating people in such a way as to awaken resentment, and we can see the points at which the vicious circle could be broken. Such understanding gives us power to free ourselves and fellow man, and wisdom about public policy.

Or to illustrate from an area in which further work needs to be done. Many people—even "experts"—talk as if there were such an entity as sex experience about which judgments can be made that hold for all such experiences. But sex in human beings is not just "natural," it is an activity interfused with culture (meanings) and a mode of human relationship. Depending upon the intentionality with which it is performed (and perceived) by the persons, it is a different experience.

Some sex acts are acts of aggression and domination, some are attempts to bolster a weak ego, some are driven by the passion of tension release (from overbusyness as well as from glands), some sexual intercourse is celebrative. Phenomenologically understood, these are not the same experience, for a quite different mode of existence and intersubjectivity result.

### Step IV—Sensing the Inner Moving Within This Length of Life World

As I stand alone at night along a beach of restless waters, looking up into the dark roundness faintly interrupted by a Milky Way, I am, but what is the world I am *in*? Is there an Inner Moving . . . that also moves me? And what are its intentions me-award?

How do I differ from the things of this world? Is this difference the best clue I can get as to the goings-on of the Encompassing Mystery in which I participate? What do I touch when I touch Presence? What is happening when I hear an answering cry from another Thou?

When I have an important experience, is that all it is? Or is there present in it a Transhistorical which will be helping form many other situations.

As my conscience reveals to me my mishandling of life, is there any Truth—both enduring and becoming—with which I can be transformed into desirable human? Is there anything I *believe in*?

Are there traces of a path through the darkness that would be a realizing journey for my one life on earth?

I cannot evade these mystical, ontological question-hungers. I cannot avoid theoanthropologizing. Catching simultaneously some revelation of the inmost formings of man (anthropo)

97

and of God (theo). So on to—
the Depths. To the Innermost Moving
the Transhistorical
the forming energies which make the human

In phase two, phenomenologizing is concerned to examine the pattern, the architectonic of a particular experience and life world.

In phase three we are going for the forming energies which make the human not only in this particular event, but in all situations. To the something going on which makes this a universe of alivenesses rather than a void, and transmutes a body into a person. This may be referred to as the Transhistorical—meaning by that, not that it is *above* history, but that it is not confined to just this one situation. In a world of volcanic energies that are ceaselessly becoming and revealing themselves into us, "transhistorical" suggests that there is a Moving that creates a humanity holding together all men.

We are after the primordial forming real of the universe in which we live, the ecology of the human, the "game" which creates humanity, an understanding story of origination and of how opposites are made into one. So that men may be united by the foundations of existence.

Many of us are indebted to Martin Buber for his discovery that the structure and dynamic of human life is I-Thou. Gabriel Marcel has offered glimpses into the forming of human reality by his report of what it means to be *with* rather than alongside other people, of the mystery of Presence, of the humanizing which comes with creative fidelity. Heidegger has posited that the essential nucleus of man—without which we would not be man—is concern. Concern about his outcome, about whether he realizes or muffs his possibility. And for increasing numbers today all over the world, man is viewed as a freedom. As a *subject*, and not first of all an object.

A moment when such an insight comes at us out of a lived moment may become a landmark occasion. To some degree a new existence begins for us and those we care about. From that point on, we have a new sensitivity to events and people. We use the insight of this particular moment to interpret many events which otherwise might be very opaque and mixed up. From that point on, no matter how far we wander, we still remain in touch. For we have been present when the Forming Momentum which is the essential becoming human process, was documented before our very eyes. What can happen in the third phase of phenomenologizing is this important. Particularly if lifted up in communal celebration.

## VISIONING

Intense perception and meaning produces visioning.

An inscape of powerful beauty comes at us. Thoroughly absorbed, we enter into it until its pattern and power reside in us. A dream mighty of wings carries us beyond the actual into what is not yet, but for us is being. We vision the struggle of humanity of which we are now agents. We may not be much, but the cause we serve is tremendous.

After years of experiences and learning, a top-rate mind visioned the evolutionary struggle of which we are now agent—

"The picture of man's evolution is not that of a huddled community waiting to be eaten, but that of explorers always learning how to live beyond the fringes. . . .

It means the survival of wing and brain, of the most adaptable, the most enduring, the most anticipatory, the most enjoying, the most diversely communicating with the universe." [1]

In visioning, we value not only *a moment,* but a *pattern* and *length* of life world.

[1] John Platt, *The Step to Man* (New York: John Wiley, 1966), p. 172.

We connect present experience with other experiences and meanings, with other people's experiences and their interpretations of them. Particularly with the internal events of people who we feel have lived life intensely, simply, productively.

And we persist in looking at fascinating beauty *and* power so that it becomes resident grace within us. Our attention is solely *upon what is*. We are not asking how we will use it, or how it would reconstruct and save our lives. We are appreciatively enfolding it, realizing its nature, feeling its significance. We come back at a deeper level to the *essential* in the experience we have had. In more traditional language, we are in contemplation.

One aid to such realizing is to start putting what we sense into memorable form. Write the poem, the contemplation, the liturgy; paint the picture, sing the song, do the symbolic act that expresses the grace that came into us. Just one memorable phrase or image may enable a meaning to endure through a lifetime.

The very process of arting gives us both time and a method of contemplating. And the emerging product keeps awakening further depths of realization—just as our speaking sentences are partly formed by our hearing what we have already been saying. Just as an artist develops his conception by beginning to paint rather than beginning with a fully grown picture in his mind.

But even at best, we realize not a highway, but the traces of a path, intimations of a trail.

## THE ROLE OF THIS CHAPTER IN MAKING CELEBRATION

We have presented disciplines of the phenomenological method by which we transform lived moments into culture.

100

In step one of phenomenologizing, we are essentially French Impressionist painters—able to sense the pulsing energies and nuances of color in the scene before us, and translate this landscape into immediacy and pure intensities juxtaposed so as to make each more vibrant and revealing.

In the second action of phenomenologizing, we are a Cézanne —able to transform the details of a particular world before us into a pattern that presents the mode of togetherness and mutual influencing that is going on. So that the belonging and the birthing leaps out to others through patterns of relationship and modulations of color.

In step three, we are a Van Gogh—totally absorbed in the swirls of energy that create this world; able to recreate that energy in definite brush strokes. So that we participate in the Forming Real.

We have emphasized that celebration comes out of freshly lived moments, vivid encounters and experiences, events in life as it is going on now.

"Working up" a celebration therefore begins with phenomenologizing some lived moment, encounter, experience, event. We then have a clearer and developed possession of what we have to celebrate. The real has been present to us, and we are rooted in it. But also we are stretching toward horizons.

How to phenomenologize is therefore basic equipment for enterprising celebration. It may be done elaborately or simply; in dialogic conversation, and in individual writing, arting, and "entering into" thought.

This present chapter is therefore pivotal for the enterprise of constructing and leading contemporary celebration.

# EXPLORATION I

As a boy I can remember playing "Home Sweet Home" on my harmonica in a lively manner. I raced through it at times much like a band might speed through "Dixie." It was a happy tune but it never evoked the depth of feeling that welled up in me years later when I watched a scene built around the same song in a Japanese movie called "The Burmese Harp." Tears still come to my eyes when I let myself enter into this particular scene.

The picture was built around the experiences and feelings of a small group of Japanese soldiers in Burma during the last few weeks of the war and the early period of their surrender before they were returned home. It began when this group was retreating and they knew that either death or capture was imminent. The Japanese military machine had broken down and they could not count on any support or supplies. There were advancing American and British troops in the vicinity that might catch up with them at any moment. Yet there was obviously affection and a close feeling of camaraderie among these soldiers which startled me since I had been fed a diet of American war movies as a youth that depicted the Japanese soldier as either a fool or a sadist. One of the soldiers, Kushima, carried a small harp with him that he would strum as they made their way through the jungle, and the others would join in singing as he played.

As it was getting dark they entered a small Burmese village which had been vacated by the natives. The Japanese soldiers were somewhat happy that they did not have to encounter the natives, and there was some horseplay as they bedded down in one of the huts for the night. Suddenly in the distance they heard the noises of the approaching Allied soldiers. The horse-

102

play was quickly replaced by panic and then a quick rush of activity to get their guns and prepare for the coming battle. Suddenly they realized to their horror that the ammunition cart which they needed had been left in the middle of the clearing, leaving them without their ammunition and risking that it would explode if hit by a bullet. The enemy was too close for them to run out and get it. Their only chance was to act as though they had not seen the Allied troops. Kushima and two other soldiers walked out of the hut, laughing as if they had been drinking. Kushima climbed up on the cart and began to play his harp. As he played "Home Sweet Home," the others sang in Japanese and pulled the cart back behind the hut. He played the song much slower than I had been used to hearing it, with many beautiful interweaving and flowing harmonies underneath the simple melody.

The second that they got behind cover, they stopped their singing abruptly, passed out the ammunition, and began peering out tensely into the darkness trying to see the approaching soldiers. They were relieved that they had their ammunition, but they were trapped and obviously frightened.

At this point, as the hustle inside the hut died down, a very strange and powerful thing gradually evolved. They were first bewildered by a strange noise coming from outside that they could not make sense of. As they listened in a frightened manner, tense and ready to fire, this noise turned into a kind of humming. Slowly as dark shapes began to become visible, all over the fields in an overwhelming number and strength, you could hear the American and British soldiers singing softly but with strength. They were standing up, walking slowly forward, holding their rifles at rest, and joining in the song where the Japanese had left off. They were responding to the music of the Japanese harp player.

The bewilderment of the Japanese soldiers turned to relief,

103

and they began to re-enter the music with their voices and harp. As the Allied soldiers moved into clear focus, there was a welling forth of the powerful and dignified chorus, with its words sung in unison: "Home, home, home sweet home, There's no place like home. . . . There's no place like home."

The music and its powerful statement of mankind's deep craving for peace and family had done what the soldiers were individually powerless to do. It had bridged the fear, hatred, and terror of their individual situation and evoked the humanity of these men. Neither side had to kill the other, and the Japanese could stop fighting with dignity. God, as the Christ, through the medium of music was releasing man into his deepest existence. Even now I can feel joy well up in me as I feel again the reality of this life-affirming and liberating process.

—Dr. Ross Snyder, Jr.

# EXPLORATION II

I have but a few brief years
   to become a truth

To understand myself
   rather than remain muddled
To light up the structures of my life
   with meanings that appear through the darkness

I have but a few brief years
   to achieve style and accent
Rather than remain multiple
   waves of sensations and happenings

Fleeting years
   to become
A truth man is meant to be
   in my own particular way.

To achieve significant form
   myself as a work of art—even though not perfect
A wisdom
   not just opinions

# 7.

# The Celebrative Style
# of Theologizing

In a process world, the method which we use in constructing meaningful world has much to do with the final product. So we ask, "What is the *style* of *celebrative* theologizing?"

## A MEANINGS THEOLOGY

Celebration theology is essentially a meanings theology.

The very purpose of celebration is not to inculcate a particular dogma in verbal form, but to awaken and let burgeon the meaning which will form the speaking word . . . in whatever situation the celebrants find themselves. And is the multidepth of the word when it is spoken. Meaning precedes the verbalism which is used to symbolize and firm it up. Primal theology is therefore meanings, rather than words. Meaning is "experiential fullness."

106

Therefore we are always concerned to get people phenomenologizing event and lived moment, rather than imprinting them with our conclusion. We invite them to come through the journey toward symbolized meaning which we have taken.

Meaning calls people to exist themselves—to blossom and be, to stand out in some distinctiveness, to live with anticipatory resoluteness. Unless our theology actually does this, we do not have a meanings theology—no matter what its form.

So of all people, the celebrative theologian is concerned that the central word used is truly symbol for the people celebrating—that it calls up meaningful experiential content rather than being just another flash in "prattly conversation." Yet we are constantly being tempted to fall back into the weary cliché or the prevelant "in-word" which allows us to bypass an exciting journey of *feeling-thinking* and arrivals of meaning. The word must be rooted in some lived moment, and its utterance must occur as life world is being formed.

A vivid meaning is very complex, and any one set of words will catch only some of it—often malignantly simplify it. Since life is so complex that no one phrase can present its full content, we will use a pluralism of symbolizing. Hoping that the full poetry of the present will be expressed by a cluster of symbols rather than by just one, and not only in words, but in various modes of artistic design.

Every important meaning is not just one simple thing—such as a dictionary definition. Love, for instance, is not merely "denying yourself for others," nor instinctual pleasuring by the Id, nor being a Good Samaritan. Among other things, it is two or more people who in mutual respect live as coexistence. It is creative fidelity to each other's growth as person. It is willingness to appear to the other person. It is delight in awareness of common destiny. Like every fundamental of life, to capture

107

our imagination a productive meaning has to be stated in three different ways, in three synonyms, in three nuances, that give the meaning semantic space and design.

"Three illuminations came to open my life."

Since it emphasizes meaning, celebrative theologizing is almost excruciatingly concerned with the right use of words, and the use of the most productive ones. It spends hours trying out which symbols most accurately document and profoundly evoke reality.

Which word or symbol we apply to a lived moment makes a different world in which we have to live. So we must continue to discover—out of our common contemporary life—new words for many of our meanings. For the words which one era in civilization had available to discern and name an experience may not be the symbolizing which another age can understand. Nor even be the most accurate. Yet the *meaning* which a word or phrase was attempting to symbolize may be a passionate hunger. So we also need to understand the fullness of the ancient words. And a great word of a civilization ought not be cheapened or violated by trying to force it to mean whatever we want it to.

A meanings style of theologizing, by its very nature, moves into convictional belief with considerable passion. Meaningful world is not a matter of detached cool indifference. The good in the world which we celebrate is usually in a most precarious position—in need of those who, believing in it, hurl the substance of their lives to help it come into power rather than disappear. There are enemies of the people, there are things to be hated and defeated. There are distinctions in value. The function of all art (and celebration is the highest form of communal art) is to clarify and intensify what we sense in the world and project in our imagination. So we will be clarifying

108

our frustrations, rages, defeats, crippling ambiguities and sinnings which diffusely slumber until they break out as monsters, *and* our convictional truth.

There is hardly a greater joy or affirmation of ourselves than to be a participative member of a group voicing and delighting in strongly held, communally treasured belief and vivid experiencing of it in action.

Convictional belief, however, is not the same as fanaticism or dogmatic imposition. For as William James has pointed out, healthy belief includes doubt—the knowledge that there are other alternatives, and within the belief itself there are openings into further explorations. And the mood of celebration rather than being a propagandistic rally, is a delightful lifting up of the journey through very concrete existence by which the belief came into some consummation. And this testimony is invitation to others to go on from there.

A *meaning* is not peripheral to the self. A meaning touches and textures the quivering pulse of the self system. Like a conviction it is a wager on a certain quality existence.

## ARTISTIC AS WELL AS LOGICAL FORMS

Celebrative theologizing symbolizes its meanings more in terms of artistic forms than logical forms.

Both are necessary. But the image carries more of the originating fullness and more of the forming energies toward future, than does a logical proposition. By very nature, art is concerned with intensifying, transforming, creating forms that vibrate with significance. Art holds together in one field contrapuntal forces that are still battling it out with one another.

Such theologizing is not against the structuring and interconnections which logical minding brings. But that is secondary process, not primary process. *Contemporary* theology is

109

more an organism of imagery than it is propositional statements.

## THE EVOCATIVE HUNCH

Celebrative style of theologizing tends to emphasize the fruitful hunch, rather than a vast system of thought. "Hunch" is used in order to emphasize that *celebrative* theological affirmation

comes from encounter and experiencing, rather than from secondhand reading. It is not coming merely from somebody else, it has a heavy investment of our identity and the content of our consciousness.

has only *partly* appeared. A hunch is a becoming image rather than a completed proposition. An apparition not yet thoroughly placed in context.

is a product of *all* the available energies of our consciousness, not just a part of us. A hunch is an *"intuitive premonition."*

is felt as incompleted action. It cries to be tried out. We are in profound dis-ease when we deny it a chance to become what it wants to be. The pregnant image and metaphor is already beginning to grow, organismic life is burgeoning and incorporating the environment into its structure and impetus.

expects leaps and transformations.

Such style is indigenous to reaching toward a theology through the concrete.

A few experiences—recurringly significant, thoroughly explored, symbolized and arted into unforgettable culture forms —are more important than a synthesizing survey of generalities. And this cycle of transformations—lived moment into meanings and symbol, symbol and meanings into embodiment

110

in persons, selfed bodies suffused with meanings transformed into intersubjectivity and a People—spirals and cumulates, but never comes to a finished system. The journey continues to have unexpected vistas, fresh starts, new conversations.

The resulting theology is therefore a leaping flame rather than a structure.

Suppose the hunch hits us

That God is a Presence?

That we (though but in the bud) are a personal Logos
—a wisdom (able to sense, symbolize, interpret, and order life worlds)
—a love (able to make persons present to us and we a part of them)
—a desire to become manifest (to be a being-in-the-world here and now)
—a troth which cannot be turned aside by suffering

and we have come to this by juxtaposing our life and that of Jesus of Nazareth? [1]

That Christ is a mode of being in the world that takes into itself what is going on and transmutes it into new possibility, incarnating in tough situations futures that are being ignored or crucified? And we are meant to be little Christs? [2]

That the Holy Spirit is a corporate phenomenon in the act of uttering love in a language which all men everywhere can understand?

That a *human* being is continuously transforming fate into destiny?

---

[1] The booklet "The Authentic Life: Its Theory and Practice," published by the Friends General Conference, 1520 Race Street, Philadelphia (1968), develops the context of this hunch.

[2] See pages 191-99 in *Young People and Their Culture* (Nashville: Abingdon Press, 1969), for fuller statement.

## "FIELD" THEOLOGIZING

Celebrative theologizing is driven by the impulse to constitute world, and place around it a supporting world. Its language will refer to life worlds, rather than to objects.

It is for this reason that the possession of an organizing nucleus (the evocative hunch) is so crucial. And that we focus upon the *field of energies* which is forming the world.

This kind of theologizing—since it is processing a field—will not form its convictional insights by a linear progression of first establishing a doctrine of God, then deducing a doctrine of man, then a doctrine of the church, etc. Rather, these all develop simultaneously with one another. Not as separate items but within a feeling for a motif and modulations of color vibrancy.

It has been recognized for some time that any one of the classical theological categories carries within it the quality of all the other categories. But celebrative theologizing is going in for new method and new categories (yet to be developed) which are more in harmony with the method and language of existential phenomenology than of Platonic philosophy. It is going after the pattern and relationships of the forces determining an event, rather than trying to climb up a ladder of abstractions.

This approach takes more seriously what were once called "penultimates." In a field theory approach to constructing a theology, God is understood by going through a multiverse field composed of our encounters with and understandings of events such as—

Love-power-justice
Freedom–expressive spontaneity
Communication
Intersubjectivity

What is a person? Existence? What does it mean to be a
*human* being?
Particularly as we undergo these as epochal events which we
value most.

Theology is always a theology of culture. Now meaning that
a theology can be adequately stated only in terms of all the
culture forms which a civilization develops (see Chapter 5).
The culture of a People—not merely its doctrinal summaries
—is its theology. For example, the expected life biography of
a person within a culture is an important theological statement.
And it is not necessarily deduced from the logic of a few
theological definitions.

Much of celebrative theologizing therefore swirls into
"organs of culture" such as great ways of being in the world,
paradigms of relationship, insight into depths of wonderment.

Until a theologian has worked through culture forms, his
theology is abstract, ethereal, naïve.

Field theologizing enables us to escape the superficial slogan
and cliché. Disciplined phenomenologizing enables us to escape
culture religion.

It is presently popular to refer to the "Lord of the Dance"
with the assumption that this phrase can be a primary symbol
of the God Christians worship. But in celebration with Christian style, we participate—not in a *dancing god*—but in *a
god leading an enterprise moving through a wilderness.* He
is a God on a journey—building up highways, opening up new
ventures and new horizons. He is an ever-becoming God whose
style is eschatological—with evolutionary developmental
momentum.

In contrast, the very nature of a dance is that it ends up in
the same space in which it started.

A great lot of pulsing and climax of orgasm may have
happened, tensions have been temporarily released; but no

113

stride forward into new country has taken place. God's tabernacle is safely circumscribed and stationary—it has not been moving into new territory. (Ironically both happenings and traditional church services fit this description.) The flesh of Egypt has once more danced in the evening fires of the golden calf, until it drops surfeited with itself.

Zorba is not a Christian. We can admire his ability not to let disaster get him down. But he does it by disconnecting into sensations created by his own body and a world shrunk to himself. He declares a moratorium rather than a new creation.

Celebration is fully human existence, not a blow-off. Celebration is the exuberance of creation, the thrust of new life coming up through the crust of what has been, a growing plant cracking apart hard earth as it shoots upward from a seed. Celebration is the "running walk" of those who reach for the beyond, not a self-exuding circling in location.

The denial of the dance as the most fundamental image of God's process and of celebration is no rejection of dancing as one of the art forms by whose expressive spontaneity we call up depths and celebrate movement. But creation and cumulative journey are the basic metaphors of life—not dancing.

Nor are the carnival and the clown useful images of what celebration is. Celebration is not escape from responsible relationships and a personal center—a prolonging of disaffiliation and transient tribalism. It is rather a converging attention upon the exuberant real as it establishes a melodic curve of behavior (as in Bonhoeffer's structure of the ethical life).

## TIME GESTALTED

Celebrative theology gestalts time into one burgeoning possibility that is present with presentational immediacy. It is not primarily concerned with the linear progression of chronological time, ticking off first a past, then a present, then a future. And assuring its members that they live in one to the exclusion of the others.

Meaning-densed time is a one energy pattern of future-past-present.

But since all print is linear, even that way of putting it betrays the reality. However with such a formulation, we do symbolize that human consciousness is *constituting* and not a bit of nature which can be measured by chronological time. A celebrative consciousness is busy putting together a world to live toward and into. A particular world which no other human being has ever before put together in quite this way and with these materials.

At the same time human consciousness recognizes paradigms —patterns of encounter through which new and old meanings of life break through to us with such an impact that an inscape which is now, has been, and will be, becomes a structure of existence-for-us.

In a developing world and a consciousness whose nature is movement, we can act meaningfully only from within a "piled-up" story. The future must get connected with what we have come out of; the present is the narrow pass through which we go into existence or nonexistence (and so is the jumping-off place, not the middle).

Only with such a *Gestalting* of time can we live as anticipatory resoluteness.

So it is not that we need a theology of hope, but that we cannot theologize without hope, i.e. a sensing of possibility (or source of possibility) that is even now present in what we are involved in.

## INTERSUBJECTIVE

Celebrative theologizing is dialogic theologizing and communal event. The Great Conversation about things that matter most has been going on for centuries. And now it is our turn.

"Intersubjective" means that we become *aware of otherness*. We encounter centers of perceiving that see differently than we do, we bump into wills that are trying to do things to the world which we inhabit. We hear one another. We sense that we have to take account of one another in order to have a world. Even that we are bound together in a common fate and destiny which cannot happen unless we together move and are together saved. We must become a mind and a society, for we are completions of one another.

So we theologize within a common enterprise of world-forming. We become an interconnected circle of people who believe one another to be fully human. We become a multiplet sensorium and minding of lived moments. By dialogic theologizing and communication we create significant symbol, we celebrate significant symbol.

"Intersubjective" means also that these transactions are from the inner-personal centers, and not just from the "how to do" instrumental regions of our personalities. The existence situation of each person is being voiced and heard—the wonder, delight, despair, sense of destiny, hope, perceivings of "lived space for me." To considerable degree we are sharing words of our own inner speech by which we value, choose, hold to a course. We are not just quoting authorities, but are dealing out words right now being formed by our true subjectivity.

Intersubjective theologizing is theologizing in order to exist —with special emphasis upon being in tune with one another in a world big enough for all of us to live in as home and habitat. We theologize in order to live as coexistence.

116

# EXPLORATION

### The Image
### in My Consciousness

I feel a tug
   on my line
      that means "this is real"
But I can't see it.
Then a shadowy swirl begins in the depths
It keeps coming and forming
   through the more lighted layers
A turtle green body
   finally breaks into the air
      at the point where sky meets water.

-2-

An image is a broad V of golden geese
   swimming on a blue lake in russet autumn.
Suddenly the V is startled; and
   cleaves the sky, wing to wing.

-3-

An image is a line of porpoises
   rising and diving
      toward a goal only they know
         scattering the little fishes out of the way
      totally absorbed
         in momentum
            effortless function
         delight.

117

-4-

A tidal wave of ocean
  Before self-consciousness has crawled out on dry land.

-5-

Solar hydrogen winds blowing into my face at 700,000 miles
an hour
  When I feel a pattern in the wind.

-6-

A crystal that grows in all directions
Whenever life's solution becomes supersaturated.

-7-

A helix twist of deoxyribonucleic acid on its way to becoming man.

-8-

The awesome mystery when—
  a man opens a long-closed barn door.
He has not been there for fifty years
  he tries to reassemble once-vivid acts and objects
    from the dim interior that no longer gives him a clearly
      structured clue.
And the whole barn is filled and heavy
  with the fatefulness of his life.

-9-

An image is the Holy Spirit . . . before theology has turned it
  into a cadaver.

## The Poetic

### (1)

A burst of reality
 that lingers
  in the feelings

### (2)

Feeling with your breath
It hits between your heart and your lungs
And your brain comes down
To put it into speech

### (3)

Laying bare a live wire carrying electric current
And seeing the electricity

### (4)

Momentum
Turning double somersaults
Diving headlong
Catching each swing just at the crest
Unexpectedly landing.

—in collaboration with Martha Snyder

# 8.

# Common Words Are Ontological

Celebrative theologizing makes use of two different kinds of words—the special words used by classic theology, and the pivotal words that we use in everyday talk about ourselves in this world.

If we use the classic phrases, we will freshen them with experience content from life as it is happening, and from today's mode of symbolizing important matters. The present chapter on "in" "with" "for" is representative of the other mode of theologizing. Of using words we are using all the time, but finding in them a transhistorical element which creates.

As I see it, celebration needs both kinds. Both can be revealing. They are not opposites, but complementary.

So we now explore how common words of everyday life enable us to grasp both the ontological and the everydayness.

## "IN" "WITH" "FOR"

Some of the deepest words of life are prepositions.

"In" and "of" and "with" and "for" and "in behalf of," carry much of the meaning of life for any of us.

I begin with the thought that the things of this world crave to be taken into the personal. And as the German poet Rilke expresses it, "our whole existence, the flights and plunges of our love, all fit us for this task."

This surging enterprise of all life that Rilke speaks of hit me the hardest some years back. My parents had shipped to us a little puppy dog when our boys were about three and five, and he grew up with the family and was regarded by them as a member of the family. There were times when we would be having such a good time as a family. He would want to be a part of it, he'd get in our way, he'd bark when we were talking, he'd run back and forth and back to each of us personally. And then—and this would really hurt you—often he would suddenly turn, with his tail down between his legs, walk off, and flop down over in the corner. As if to realize, "No, I can't make it." He had this desperate feeling that he wanted to be a part of the world of the personal—it was terribly attractive to him. He did the best he could, but he had mind enough to finally discover he couldn't quite make the level of human existence because he couldn't enter into the same kind of personal interaction that was going on between us.

## In

And so the word "in" has become quite important to me. And quite exciting to explore.

First of all, we are living in what could be called a sacramental universe that is in process into the world of the personal. I have already reported to you my interpretation of

121

the actions of our first dog. Well after a while we had a second dog. The first one unfortunately liked to get outdoors and after a number of years got run over by a car, and my youngest son and I had to bury him in the backyard. By this time our youngest son had gotten through college and was in medical school, and he got very interested in becoming a heart surgeon. And of course to do that you practice on dogs. One time, as he and his team were beginning a practice session, a majestic dog was brought into the room, and they spoke to him—"Get up on the table"—and he did! And that stopped them! So he brought him home. And he became a part of us. I'm sure he was the most manly gentleman I have ever met. He could do just a little bit more of actually entering into the world of the personal than the first dog. There was a gentlemanliness and a dignity in him that you respected and he respected. And he respected yours. He was just a little more "in" the personal.

Now this taking the things of the world with us into the realm of the personal is quite different from polluting the universe and using the universe for our purposes without ever regarding it as having any worth and value in and of itself. Today more and more people are becoming sensitive to the fact that there is a respectful relationship we can have with a universe that is on its way to being a part of the personal. A universe that has produced the personal is not just an object or thing to be treated in a "having and using" fashion. But is to be treated as part of a whole living story that we are a part of, and that pulls us all together. In some degree we owe our existence through time to these forms of life. We owe our continued existence to the system of life which we now call ecology. Today's man is entering into a renewed sense of being a part of a sacramental universe in which everything is interrelated. So interrelated that we now discover that when we begin to destroy an aspect of it, we are destroying the whole system. This we have a hard time understanding. So we are going to explore the word "with" after awhile.

The beginning of all life is in this little preposition "in." So on your own apply it to your everyday life as is meaningful to you. What are the things of this world that you open up *your* consciousness to and take into *your* awareness so that they live inside you the rest of your life? Who are the persons?

A few years back I went to the Presbyterian church I grew up in and met again some of the people who were growing up when I was. I spoke with a widow whose husband had just died (I had known him too), and she said, "Just six months ago on a nice beautiful evening like this Dan looked up at the moon and said to me—'Who would ever want to leave this?'" Her husband had taken into himself the beauty of the world and some sense of the total universe. In such a way that the hurting threat of death was the bereavement of no longer being able to have this world inside himself.

One of the joys of life is living long enough some places that you can take in the beauty of ocean, the beauty of mountains, the beauty of people—so that thereafter they live *in you*. Life begins to be alive partly to the degree this *inness* takes place within us.

Somewhat superficially and inaccurately we often call such "inness" a memory. A large part of me is memories. Such as memories of two youngsters I taught in high school who were making a terrifically good try in life. And then sudden death. So they no longer lived except in the memory of myself and other people who knew them. To have taken into my life the person they were has been a strength to me all my life. Within me are also the members of my family—the present one and the one in which I grew up. I have inside me still the great big hoot owls that used to come and hoot outside my window when I was a small boy. And scare me to death. I

123

have within me the thunder and lightning that used to strike the big oaks close to our house—and I always had a feeling (a queer kind of thing when you look at it rationally) that God had something for me to do in this world of ours and nothing would ever happen to me until I got it done.

All these things and persons that we have taken *into* ourselves finally are what we are. Some of the problems of life today is that some people are so empty, or have taken into themselves so much of hatreds and enmities that they are hardly able to be persons.

So "in" seems to be one of these crucial prepositions that is the very nature of our life here. And if that's true, I keep saying to myself, "Look, why don't we make use of this gift instead of being so rushing about that we deny it?"

I have a hunch that you never are able to become a person until someone takes you *into* himself. Every infant born in this world of ours cannot become a *person* until he is taken *into* the consciousness of the mother and father—and dwells there in such a way that the child becomes aware that he is *in* the father and mother. We have this strange power of birthing one another by taking one another into our consciousness and awareness. And so acting and talking that the other is aware that they live in us. Probably the only way we achieve self-consciousness is to first of all be aware somebody else is aware of us. Having that awareness we are then able to become aware of ourselves and to be personal. I keep meditating on this— that we have this mysterious power all our lives of birthing other people into a new level of existence, to the degree that we take them into the consciousness with which we form worlds. And they know that we do.

To have nobody around from whom you get a message— "yes, you exist," "you are," "I'm aware of you, there is something here that I take account of"—is the most disastrous thing

124

that can happen to anybody. Such children are lacking in a sense of identity and therefore are amoral—as the autistic child is. Now there are many causes of autism in a child, but often the autistic child has never been taken into the awareness and consciousness and the mind and the heart of the father and mother. And because that has never come off, they themselves are unable to be aware of themselves except as blind desire. They cannot love anybody else because they themselves were not taken early enough into someone else's consciousness and awareness. They are most difficult kind of people to bring back into humanness.

We have so much abundant evidence that we do birth one another by taking other people into ourselves, and that when other people don't take us into themselves we remain very immature, very desperate, very dehumanized.

At a conference in 1968, the adults and the young people we were working with all agreed that they were being treated as numbers in their everyday life. I'll never forget the high-school boy who got up after we had pointed out all the things trying to make us dehumanized and said, "Well, I feel very good about myself; I respect myself very much. I am very, very worthy. I am 5621." And he sat down. He had just made the most eloquent speech during the whole discussion!

There is a terrific amount of dehumanization going on in our schools, in our industries, in our families because we don't have time to take each other into our awareness. Because we get so much feedback that nobody is taking us into his heart and mind. "I'm here merely as something to be shaped." "Other people are so indifferent to me that nobody thinks I'm worth interiorizing."

The more I examine the word "in" the more I see the whole meaning of life. Certainly it is one of the post potent, powerful words we can possibly experience.

125

## With

I come then to "with" as another everyday reality that ought to be more everyday than it is.

I'm indebted to Gabriel Marcel for helping me become fascinated with the dimensions of "with." Gabriel Marcel was a man who looked at the ordinary events of life in order to discover the meaning of his life. He felt that this was the way that you found it out. Don't disregard the little events of life. If only we could see it, they have packed in them the secret of life.

For instance—like a lot of other commuters—when Marcel traveled the train to Paris he stuck his nose in a newspaper and kept it there. Or took out his notebook and scribbled down his thoughts. One morning, however, instead of reading his newspaper, he turned and began to talk to the man sitting beside him. That was so different from the other kind of riding which he had previously done that his mind kept working on what had happened. He formulated the question—"What does it mean to live *with* rather than *alongside* somebody?" A theology evolved out of this simple experience—being with somebody as contrasted with being alongside them.

So the word "with" is an interesting preposition likewise. It's very closely associated in meaning with "in," but it also brings more meanings.

What happens when somebody is *with* you rather than alongside you? Well, this table can be alongside me, but it can't be *with* me. This may be because I have no knowledge whether there is any sensitivity and awareness going on inside it. But at any rate, it remains to me forever external object. I cannot be *with* a table. Whereas it is possible, if I'm sensitive enough, and we can talk honestly enough, that you can penetrate into my mind and I can penetrate into *your* mind so

126

that we become an intersubjectivity. We can *together* create something. When a husband and wife look at their firstborn they have this deep sense of being *with* each other in a way they never had previously. So that *with* as contrasted to "alongside" means that we have become permeable to each other, something of each other does dwell in each of us, and there is joint creation of new life.

## Presence

The basis of "with" is presence. I hope to be a presence to you at the same time I encounter you as presence.

Marcel came to this discovery through another personal experience. After the First World War, he was part of the government staff whose business it was to go around and talk to the families of men who were either still missing persons or word had finally come through that they had died. In the government files these men were "cases." They were names and numbers and descriptions of another case to be handled. But Marcel noticed when he talked with the wives or mothers or sons or daughters of these persons, there was something quite different in their minds when that person's name was mentioned than was in his mind. For one who had loved them and lived *with* them, this person was a *presence*—not an object or a case to be completed.

A presence—who knows how to define what we mean by it? There are probably only a few times in your life when you were aware of some other person as presence—really! Most of the time we enjoy or don't enjoy having another person around, but once in awhile they are a presence to us. We become aware that they are Mystery—a layer upon layer whose beginnings only we touch. Back and back and back of that there is still depth of them to be found.

127

A Presence is also something that you would not violate or profane. You don't want to reach out and shape it because you respect *its* power to shape itself. You don't reach out to try to tell it what to do because you sense "here is another center of valuing—and life project. I want to treat it as a subject, not an object. I can offer information, I can offer my experience, but I must never invade as with a foreign army such a center. I must not—as I might easily do with piece of wood—cut it up. For this is a human dignity—something infinitely mysterious that partakes of the mystery of the universe and of God's mystery. "Here is an image of God. Here is a spark of the Divine, which originatively is of God and not of me."

Sometimes when I perform a wedding ceremony for students that I've known, and they come to that place where they pledge their troth—their faithfulness to each other—and they turn and face each other and repeat the vows, the whole space around them is filled with an intense sense of Presence. Both of them are aware of each other as a Presence—and of an event of Mystery happening—in a way that normally people are not. You are in the Presence of something sacred when you are aware of this kind of mystery of Presence.

Presence, then, is what we essentially are. And what God is. Once in awhile we are sensitive enough to catch another as Presence and then we live *with* them rather than alongside them.

This is a father's report of a landmark event in his life.

"It was a very unsettling period for me because there was conflict in my church. There were nagging questions about the church and whether I was meant to be a minister. And where was I going in life anyway? And the late winter doldrums were hitting me real hard. My wife and son had gone out for the afternoon leaving four-year-old David and myself home together.

David went in to lie down on our bed for his afternoon rest time. He chattered quietly to himself. I mused, listening to him. I started trying to work on a paper due for class, but I typed only a few minutes. My mind wandering, unable to concentrate, I went in to be with him for awhile. I lay down next to him. He cuddled up next to me and smiled his infectious smile. He reached over and fingered my shirt. And then for a few minutes we talked about little things.

A comfortable gladness began in me—no more brooding, just warmth. So I told David, "It makes me so happy to be here with you." He smiled and snuggled closer. I knew he knew. And then he talked with me. "Babies don't come from Mommy's stomach, they come from her uter-er-us! And do you know where pumpkins come from? From pumpkin seeds! And do you know where baby chicks come from? Out of eggs!" He told me about talking about all these things at nursery school. He was sharing things very important to him.

Tears, real tears, welled out and streaked my cheek. Tears of happiness, contentment, gladness, father-hood. This little guy was really giving his knowledge and experience of life in this intimate quiet rest time. He heard my words of caring and he re-sponded, responded in the most meaningful symbols he knew by telling me of the most important things he had heard that week. At his level he was the-ologizing. Communicating the source of his being—

129

how he came about. And the joy of existing that his small world allowed him.

In his love-gifting there was meaning. Self came alive *with* another. In his sharing there was trust, there was excitement, there was laughter and of course questions, questions, questions. But to David I was a real person. And it is great to be a person to someone else, especially if he is only four years old."

## COMMUNICATION

This is what we mean by "withness." And it makes clear to us how much *communication is a part of* the life of being with people.

And there can't be very worthwhile communication unless each of us has something to communicate. Part of the impact in the experience just related comes from the four-year-old's sense of something very, very, important in life. And now his dad was willing to listen to it. For a child to succeed in sharing something very, very important with his father is a treasured occasion of humanness.

I have only a few times when this intensity of communication takes place. But without such events, we never know what communication really is. Most of the time, we're sharing information with one another. Most of the time we're giving orders to one another or refusing to take orders from one another. We dwell too much in feeble and futile attempts at communication that come from being "alongside." Particularly in homes, we could have more quality communication.

A church group of parents had been meeting regularly during a year, and I had been with them several times. I particularly remember one evening when, as a couple came in,

130

they said to me, "You know after the parents' meeting last week, we went home and talked until three o'clock in the morning. And we talked about things we had never been able to talk about before."

Now if that was true of a couple who got along with each other, what must be true of many marriages where probably never in their lives have they sat down and talked about important secrets about life . . . that they feel as celebratively as this boy above felt about what he shared with his father.

A contemporary church will train its people in communication.

Communication is a most important aspect of love. And it is often not present at significant levels. Between two married people, love may fall from grace into routine. It may become too exclusively defined in terms of sexual orgasm in each of them. There are not enough times of quality conversation. So the withness—even while it is faithful—does not have the fullness and the zing to it that it could have.

Let's face it—you and I are almost afraid to be quite honest with each other. We're afraid to break up the custom that all gatherings must become chitchat with the current clichés and lint of life thrown back and forth. And the usual worn-out games of relationship are played. Once in awhile, there should be a place where it's all right to go for *conversation*.

A chief gripe of young married women I know is that their husbands tell them nothing about what's happening where they work. I don't think this is being nosey and invading privacy, though it could become that. They want to co-exist with their man, and how can they unless they are let into some of his interesting experiences, the encounters that stir him up, his glimmers and expectancies about the nature of his work and where it is meaningful to him.

131

Hear, then, the conclusion: when we say "in" and "with," we are defining Christian love and the Christian style of life.

## COMBINATION WORDS

The whole life and writings of Martin Buber were an attempt to say that there are two *words of life,* and both of them are combination words. One of them is the combination I-It, and the other is the combination I-Thou. You have to live with both of them. But unless you have discovered the I-Thou combination existence then indeed life is kind of hell.

Buber went on to report further that in moments of I-Thou, we sometimes sense Presence—the presence of God at work.

It may be that such a combination situation is the best place you'll ever be able to be with and in God. So be it.

# EXPLORATION

Every new human being
  Begins in communication

         ❋    ❋    ❋

The neighborhood
  Of free selves
On the peaks
  Of existence

Related
  As free partners
In the interplay
  Of mankind

The flashing sparks
  from one pole of the battery to the other
Opening our soul
  more widely to the possible

         ❋    ❋    ❋

Not parrots
  Of conventional phrases
But makers
  Of themselves

The existing man
  Who speaks decisively
Men who selve themselves
  In the process of mutual self-revelation

         ❋    ❋    ❋

Not
  a watering down

But a clarification
in which we can meet one another

Making possible
a realm
In which we can all
meet one another

Free only so far
As the other one becomes free
Becoming ourselves only to the degree
The other becomes himself

❊   ❊   ❊

The honest
and patient
Negotiation
Of even the most rending differences

The unlimited will-to-communicate
To know the other, to hear him
To reckon with him even to the necessity
Of transforming oneself

❊   ❊   ❊

Only thus
can the genuine strength
Of man
be developed

Only thus
does the Creativity in which we participate
Reveal itself
unmasked out of the depths.[1]

[1] Adapted from Karl Jaspers' writings on communications.

# V DESIGNING
#   A CELEBRATION

# 9.

# A Multi-consciousness
# Is Functioning

We now begin to work specifically on how a celebration takes on significant form—its flow of movement and design.

Celebration is an expression of multi-centric, multi-spiraled, multi-dimensional, multi-languaged consciousness. The artist-designer-celebrator needs to understand how such consciousness functions. Adequate celebration awakens such multi-consciousness.

## A) MULTI-CENTRIC

We are indebted to William James for the insight that at any one moment consciousness is not one thing, but a pluralistic complexity; not a flat surface but a centered universe extending out in all directions.

Every awareness has a focus of attention—but also has subliminal depths and concentric ripples. From these margins and depths, elements may invade and supplant the existing center. And at that instant we change. Because what we par-

137

ticularly pay attention to in the complexity determines what we become.

Most of the time we are not consciously aware of this outer geography of our awareness. But these contents are there. By changing the intention and symbols with which we scan the total, they may come up from dimness into clarity, from periphery to center, from comparative powerlessness to ruling vitality.

The meaning of any experience depends not merely upon the foreground focus of our attention, but also upon this background and surroundings. The focus would have no meaning without the rest of the "universe" (which is why verbal intellectual clarity by itself is so impotent). The involved background, the far-expanding plural complexity of the total consciousness, is operating—whether we know it or not.

Our conscious attention tries to live with the fiction that this total can be ignored and even thrown away. But our consciousness is a multi-centric sphere. All of it—not merely the highlighted center—is helping determine outcome. And it is a rich source of further possibility.

Such total consciousness, therefore, is the unit of communication, of growth, of celebrative existence. And calls for multilanguages to express its complexity as a global whole.

## B) MULTI-SPIRALED

Human consciousness is multi-spiraled.

Formerly we would have said "layered," but that verbalism tends to put in our minds a misleading picture. We then tend to break up consciousness into separate parts—a condition which exists in the mentally ill. "Spiral" suggests a momentum in which all parts participate, and that all are interpenetrated with the same pervading quality, texture, color. And further

138

—all are slightly different the next time when they stand in a new lookout and encounter a somewhat changed bit of world.

In a spiral, a totalizing is constantly going on. Consciousness is a spiraling flame rather than the line upon line, brick upon brick of established building. The whole of it keeps moving into new possible world and existence.

The spiral is composed of "preconscious," "conscious" and "emergent" or feedforward consciousness.

## Preconscious

The spiraling begins with constituting consciousness as preconscious.

Preconscious refers to that organization of consciousness that functions in the immediacy of encounter with some aliveness in the world. In any experience, our attention is *centered.* Around that center of attention is a wealth of details and mood that we do not possess consciously, but which determines much of the meaning. This preconscious may be a mood left over from a previous experience.

Preconscious is a mobilization of our total body of sensibility —residues of experiences, life project as of that moment, established modes of being in the world, stock of symbols and words, relationships and troths, feelings about self-in-this-world, biology. The project of this total body tunes in to what is before us, and organizes it as meaningful world.

Preconscious is a better concept than the more common "unconscious."

First of all, the emphasis is upon preconscious as originative, creative source. "Preconscious" is nearer to Jung's concept of the unconscious than Freud's, but includes both.

As in Jung's unconscious, the preconscious is an ocean of life from which many shapes emerge. It is not to be feared, but to be nurtured. It is a moreness than the person now actualizes. Within it are energies working for its own transformation. It is not disconnected from the conscious (except in ill-health), part of it is on its way to becoming conscious. Likewise residues from the conscious enter into the next preconscious—affecting its preceptual tools, relational abilities, quality of feelings.

While it is not disconnected from the conscious and part of it is on its way to becoming conscious (and changed by the interaction that then goes on), the *significant* possibility in it may not get to the center of symbolization. For the preconscious is constantly tyrannized by previous feeling mobilizations and previous symbolizations. Particularly by verbal counters that are no longer symbols of what is in the preconscious—or symbolize a past already without power or actually repulsive. Verbal counters that do not accurately symbolize the environment with which we must now make life world are a menace.

The preconscious is also constantly being dehumanized by deep-lying rage, hostility, resentment, desire to dominate and have, anxieties, dreads and despairs, fears, unresolved guilts, defensive and masking games, immediate pleasure pangs, etc. All these repressed contents may break out in power any minute.

## Conscious Consciousness

In the immediacy of any instant, our consciousness is largely preconscious. But within is a more intensely sensed and verbally lighted center. This latter may be thought of as conscious consciousness.

Influencing goes back and forth between these two regions. The movement is not just in one direction—from the preconscious into the conscious—but two-way. It is important to consciously nurture this inter-movement. (Celebration can do this particularly well.) Productive vitality comes as they co-create.

The preconscious experience is the beginning and continuing source of power. The conscious organizes experiences into persisting forms, isolates parts and studies them in detail, names the overall organization, thinks out new patterns, meta-phors an interwoven universe of meanings, organizes a self-identity. The conscious is highly verbal. It is what we usually think of as ourselves in governance of ourselves.

Now to look at its various functionings in personal life.

One function of the conscious is to select out of all that is before and in us, a centered world to which we pay particular attention and come to understand. This is a great service. If it did not happen, we probably could not act, or see anything but diffuse, buzzing confusion. We could not understand any-thing—only flood with emotion and impulse.

We give a name to this structure of forming energies which we have seen—a name which enables us to present it to our valuing and judging, bring it into conversation with many other situations which had similar structures and dynamic. And so we begin to comprehend.

"Conscious," therefore, means that we have formed a *pattern* out of the flux of streaming world. For a length of time, we now live in a dependable world with a dependable self-identity. We can be a developing continuity rather than endless somer-saults reaching for unknown swings.

By these continuing tryings for the most productive way of locating and naming the focal energies of a situation, we transcend both the first symbols we used and the lived moment itself. We look at the content and pattern of our consciousness from a standpoint other than that of our own immediate preconscious, we choose symbols in terms of a second exploration that can be more far-seeing and intelligent.

We come out of immersion in the stream of events, pause, look around, re-collect and interweave our experiences into an intended journey. We know that this is our focus, and we are not in the grip of invisible monsters.

But even as important, we have inserted them into the self-system. We identify the experiencing and its interpretation as Me. We build up an identity. Even in the very act of searching and choosing appropriate symbol, we experience ourselves as agent and as transcendence. We become in charge of our experiences and emotions, rather than obsessed by them. We can affirm them as what we intend; or purify, change, reflect them. We can break a vicious sequence of events in our consciousness.

And so arrive at wisdomed consciousness rather than mere pulsion. And that most delectable state when we know that we know, and delight in what we know. And in ourselves as knower.

Celebration is such heightened transcendence.

But we must keep clear that conscious consciousness is not the same as a mind possessing verbalisms put there by propagandists, advertizers, custom, cruel groups demanding conformity. Verbal conditioning is the worst form of conditioning —for the person all his remaining life does it to himself and his associates. And being put there apart from firsthand experiencing, reinforced by rewards and punishments coming from an un-get-at-able authority, it is almost impossible to overthrow its dominion. Throughout all history, religious groups have at times excelled at verbal conditioning.

Celebration should not fall into this sinning. It should invite *constituting* consciousness, two-way interaction between the first-hand experiencing and the symbols chosen to represent it, free play of the mind and feeling to find the best symbol.

## Emergent Consciousness

Then there is an evolutionary leap into a new mode of consciousness which might be called the consciousness which visions. Which arts life world that is not yet. A "feedforward," rather than a feedback. Creative evolutionary *imagination*.

We are talking about an evolutionary emergent—a visioning . . . imaging . . . creating the new . . . consciousness. The consciousness awakened in intersubjectivity. The consciousness which is a part of the becoming it is aware of.

To understand human consciousness, we do not so much trace its beginning stages or reduce it to chemistry. Rather we ask, what is it revealing of its possible nature in its peak moments? A nature which is then also discoverable in the preconscious.

Some sensitive minds report an encounter with the trans-historical depths of all being. As William James intellectually put it, the reaches of our private consciousness touch the margins of a vast "feeling thinking." And in the resulting explosion, all things are made new.

As D. H. Lawrence wrote, "It is a fearful thing to fall out of the hands of the living God."

## C) MULTI-BUNDLED

We may also look at human consciousness as organized in bundles of feeling, of experiences, of images, of ideas.

In any given experience, all these are the awakened content of consciousness. They come all intertwined. But to some degree, they are also regions with their own organization.

### Feeling-Intending

Personality is held together by a prevailing feeling tone. An ocean of feeling with surging tides of intention. Into this ocean pour our sensings, emotions, valuings. And from it feeling power and tone pour into all regions of the consciousness. Experiences stir up different waves of feeling, but there is also a continuing ocean.

Out of this ocean of feeling and underrivers of intention comes headlong vitality and celebration.

Feeling as we are talking about it here, is more than emotion. Feeling is from deeper depths than is emotion, is less surfacy. And so is more massive in its rhythms, more enduring over lengths of time. It is less jittery and excitable, more interfused with valuings held significant by the self, more moving into beginning ideas. Feeling is already arranging its energies and these suffused contents into image of "possibility-for-me."

### Structures of Experience

But our consciousness does not remain liquid fluidity and flow. We encounter the world and have experiences which take on structure. The dynamic, pattern, taste, of vivid experiences also become contents of the mind. Those of similar style and quality begin to cohere into a preferred pattern of experience. Those that complement and fulfill each other (and have our enthusiastic approval) become our great ways of being in the world. They become the architectonic of our self.

An experience, of course, is not apart from the other bundles of mind's content, but an organization of all of them. Every experience, for example, is suffused with a feeling-intending

144

which is dialoguing with the already "resident" bundle of feeling-intending.

An experience is a length of happenings which *have to do with us*. We have encountered something with which we have to deal. Our mind is throwing up hypotheses for action (ideas), forming imagery of possible futures, vibrating with the meanings it is manufacturing. The greater the risk, the more passionate the feeling, the more alive the self, the more strongly the experience coheres and remains a persisting shape of energy in our consciousness.

Such experiences are lived moments. They are not just a passing or boring happening. In a lived moment we become aware that we have values, want to live and find realization. We experience our self as very active.

Full-dimensioned presentation of such a lived and filled moment—and development of its richness—is the original data out of which every celebration develops. Any other way of originating a celebration is contrived and didactic.

## Image

A memorable experience leaves in the mind a *picture* of the peak moment, or of someone in the situation being forcefully person. Images are the third content and form in which our consciousness shapes itself.

A "picture in the mind" begins as a momentary perception. The forming powers of consciousness keep working away at this momentary perception until it becomes an image with which we feel, value, choose, enterprise ourselves over a period of time. The image stays within us and offers organization and energy to any succeeding moment that has similar organization.

For an image is possibility, rather than mere actuality. The

145

actual has become clarified, made more intense through heightened relationship of its parts, put into compelling design. It opens up what we can yet be, even though we are not that now. From within it, future leaps out toward us, captures our attention, evokes movement. An image is a helix of DNA on its way to becoming man!

An image reeks with immediacy and surgence. In it is momentum, and around it is horizon. So it is a form of *synthesizing* knowledge which holds together a whole field of possible existence. To learn an image is to learn a functioning whole which is capable of almost endless expansion and power to digest many situations.

A habitual vision of greatness forms a great character. Every civilization has foundational imagery which holds it together as a society. And by which it understands what happens.

One purpose of liturgy and celebration is to evoke, art, and render clear to popular understanding, great imagery of possible becoming.

### Bundles of Ideas

When most people speak of mind, they think of it as a network of ideas.

We have been trying to make clear that mind has much more content than ideas. However our mind is equipped and organized by ideas, even though it also has organization of feelings, of experiences, of images. And all these participate together in structuring the total mind.

But what is an idea?

It is a way of presenting to ourselves in most condensed, rapidly manipulatable, and combinable form the *what is* of a person, natural object, event. Together with hypothesis, "If I do this in this situation, then that will come about."

An idea, then, is a statement about how the real works, and

146

how we can best enter into creation of meaningful world. To say, "Let's go and have an ice cream cone," is not an idea (there may be one back of the suggestion), even though it meets the valuable description of an idea as incompleted action.

Ideas make possible the *principled* man—the person who can transcend the partialness of any experience or desire because he has understandings useful in many situations. And these are interconnected into an integrity. So that parts can change or drop out, but the broad understandings stay connected and grow through the due activity of the network as an organic developmental system. Learning, wise self-governance that keeps on target, civilized society, all require principled integrity.

Religion has usually insisted—and rightly—that not merely ideas but the whole consciousness is involved in the transactions of man's constituting consciousness. But still, ideas, reasoned convictions, beliefs that are articulated and tested, are part of the content of any mature religion. To deny their exclusive control and exclusive activity is not to invite man to degenerate into thoughtlessness, electronic wash of emotion, credulity, emotional followership. Ideas are not worthless baggage. And the religious enterprise of mankind must be concerned with helping form the great idea whose time to form mankind has come.

A timely great idea cannot be run-of-the-mill, nor one so domesticated that it is no longer startling. Many ideas are true, but at any one time only a few—possibly only one—have the power to awaken intense and sustained energies. We have no time for any other kind today.

The idea has to be taken up, incarnated by people who are highly visible, admired, and articulate, if it is to make impact upon the public and be understood by them. "In the begin-

147

ning," the "idea" is a lived existence rather than an articulated idea.

An idea whose time has come has power to bind people and enterprises together, interweave them into desired developmental journeys and history's continuities. It is not just another idea, but a *fresh total* of consciousness.

Western man has tended to exalt technical reason—it has made possible our use of the world to build up a high standard of living, create a world that matches the desire in our hearts. But technical reason—how to utilize objects, how to get something done—is not all that ideas are about. Ideas are important just because they present to us *what is*; enable us to recognize and identify whatever it is that we are meeting. So that we *commune* with it—understandingly. Delight and celebrate that there is such actuality in the world. Affirm that it has a right to be itself—whether it ever serves our wishes and desires or not. Such aesthetic-intellectual love of convictional truth has distinguished man at his best.

What then do we do with ideas in celebration?

Clearly the purpose of celebration is not instruction. In celebration, the bird is on the wing, not in a manual.

We can explore the multi-complexity of a great idea by getting inside the total situation out of which it came and walking around inside it appreciatively. We can hear what persons of some dimension said in their hearts as they struggled and created. Until we "own" a great idea.

Perhaps we can lead the celebrative group through the process of developing an idea. The "rightly raised" idea grows up through an experience, through tumultuous yet symbolized feeling, aided by metaphoring and creative imagination. This journey can be taken in a celebration. Thinking is not a wind blown through the mind, but transactions between symbols and actuality. Thinking is not secondhand conclusions which

148

are announced to us, but firsthand "I was there, and this mind-ing goes on in me."

Hopefully we can set in motion in the celebrative group an exuberance of growing up ideas.

## Systems of Meaning

When any one of these contents—feeling, experience, image, idea—is sensed as "This has to do with me—this is me" we have the beginning of meaning.

A full orb of meaning is all these five contents interacting and functioning as a whole.

Probably the most potent full orb of meaning is a symbolic act. For in an act, all contents of consciousness are in motion —and as fused together. "Symbolic" suggests that the act is knowingly intentional; we are asserting that *we* mean some-thing. That we are leaving the familiar city for a new land (Abraham's emigration); that of all memberships available, this particular membership (participating in the Eucharist) is the most significant, and we press forward toward it (the moment we joined an unpopular cause).

But what do we mean by "meaning"?

Meaning begins with a *felt* "this is expanding, enlivening, freeing, enabling me." Or the opposite, "this is boring me, deadening me, closing doors to desired future, cutting me off from membership." Or—as usual—confusing mixtures of these two meanings.

First of all, then, a meaning is sensing a particular action upon the self and its destiny.

*Meaning* is not something we can give to another person— it has to be made out of the contents of his consciousness and the intents of his self-system.

A verbalism—as such—has no meaning. It is only a potential

149

for meaning. It can awaken meaning only by throwing into activity the multi-bundled consciousness of the hearer. And even then, the "consumer" determines the meaning that rises up. For *meaning* is the foreseeable fate-destiny awakened in *him* by the other's input. It is not the input itself.

Further, each of us is so tied in to our fate *from within* that no one can experience *our* sorrow as we do—even though they do their best to enter into it. The sympathizer's existence is influenced by another person's experience in a secondary way. While for the person undergoing it, the actuality is primal and immediate. The latter person *is* suffering—it is his mode of *being* at the moment. Whereas the mode of being-in-the-world of his sympathizing friend is that of sympathy. And there is great difference between these two.

The second element of meaning is *relationship*. That which makes no connection with anything else is temporarily meaningless. Meaning for our life comes from *placing* ourselves in some situation and some web of humanity, and affirming that we intend this context of our life. Meaning comes with gestalting ourselves and the world around us.

### Summation

A *human* being lives in meanings, not raw event or stepped-up sensations.

A very large part of all ministry is a ministry of meanings. Of helping people develop and mobilize full-consciousness.

Celebration awakens and hurls together these five contents of consciousness: feeling-intendings, memorable experiences, images, ideas, systems of meaning arising out of the self-system.

Only situations in which our fate is involved are really meaningful world for us. Therefore in a celebration there is no point in dealing with experiences in which those present were not involved. For they immediately go into a moratorium.

150

## D) MULTI-LANGUAGED

Multi-centric, multi-spiraled, multi-bundled consciousness is multi-languaged.

Word symbols are the most obvious language with which we put these contents into significant form, and try to awaken them in others. Particularly word symbols freshly put together in metaphor, in story, in myth of creation and our people.

But symbolic deed is also a language.

Sound is a language. Music is a language.

Visual image is a language. Imagination and visioning use a very complex diffused language.

In a celebration, all these languages are talking to us, awakening us, binding us together into a society. And when it comes off, they are all joined into a one complex language of the becoming human.

## E) MULTI MODES OF COMMUNICATION

Marshall McLuhan has helped us grasp that the mind of man has been shaped by three modes of communication during his history: (1) face-to-face communication *as he is carrying on life* in a small village and in his family, (2) the printed word and reading, whereby a man's thoughts can be widely spread and examined again and again by groups of people in his absence, (3) electronic communications that are multi-sensory, and therefore "global," i.e., communicating simultaneously the whole scene all put together, and to person or group in their own habitat apart from the communicator and originating situation. This mode tends to emphasize art forms rather than logical forms of expression and communication.

These are all important ways—and necessary ways—of forming contemporary consciousness. Together they make possible a fullness never before possible. Any one of these to the exclusion of the other two misleads man about the kind of world from which revelation and relationship can come to him.

The mobilization of these three is one of the unique possibilities of present day communal celebration. One of its major strengths. This statement does not mean that every celebration *must* include electronic media, face-to-face "I-Thous," Gutenberg print. The latter is peculiarly confining and destructive of immediacy. Celebration does not consist of following a printed program, or words written down by somebody else for us to say. But also very often electronic gimmickry turns what might have been a *celebration* into an admiration occasion for the gimmickry.

We are saved if we look upon these three as *modes* of communication (and symbolization)—rather than merely eras. Particularly as means of arriving at significant symbol which is a group creation and possession. And use each when it is relevant.

We then ask questions such as, "Is there a point in this celebration when what needs to be done calls for 'original' conversation?" Talking face to face as we are trying to handle life? Dialoguing in two's or multiplets of six or total group conversation? Or in shouts and antiphon? Is it possible in this celebration to create a drama of intense group thinking, of struggle for outcome right then and there? Or perhaps more importantly, are such occasions in life, the only times celebration can authentically happen?

Surely such an uproarious power as "in situation, face-to-face with each other" communication will not be ignored in communal celebration. It is still the way mind, self, and society are born and developed.

We also need "print consciousness" communication.

To the degree that it develops searching discussion and

152

unfuzzy thinking, it helps rescue us from enslavement to crowd propaganda and hysteria. "We all feel this way very passionately, so it must be true" is an ever-present danger in any celebration. We need a mode of symbolizing and communication that will jerk us out of any such marginal world of vaporized consciousness. How to do this without destroying the atmosphere of appreciation and total absorption in the strength and beauty of what we have encountered and experienced, is high artistry. Perhaps there should be other occasions when searching thinking is the chief item of business.

And celebrations must not leave out dialogue with what authentics have said in their hearts as they struggled to make sense out of life. And on the whole this will be made possible by linear print communication. Celebration would be poor and provincial if only the expressions of the assembled group were allowed, or if so-called "contemporary" arts were the only languages. What has been achieved anyplace, anytime should be made widely and generously available in its original form—if it is relevant. For no present moment is full unless it is filled with memorable past, as well as with expectant future and actuality.

But the new electronic languages, the new media, the new modes of symbolizing and of communicating to others, will increasingly be significant in communal celebration. And they are yet largely undeveloped. In celebration's circles much hard work needs to be done to develop these vocabularies.

Particularly as we see electronic media as way of awakening the human in us and our society, rather than as instruments to manipulate people. As means of sensing fascinating meanings, as a method of theologizing with our whole consciousness, as ways of appreciation and celebration.

# EXPLORATION

The darkness is no longer total
The solid immense depths behind depths
Are being thinned out

The darkness changes
But no one source of light can be seen

All in the world begins once again
Massive, diffuse, not yet speaking its architecture
Sensed rather than seen
Totally abstract, a world without color

But photons of light
Have each traveled the world, until now
All things
Send out a fusing soft light

Not the cold stare which exposes shapes against their will
But inhering light
Graciously comes toward us
All things together

2

All flesh feels an instress of power
No longer belongs to numb sleep and the dark
But to this new pulse

Translated
Into song of birds
Who hilariously shout
That they are,
That they claim a place in the world

154

(Yet the world still belongs
To wrecked boats
And the sudden demonic
That wrecks boats)

### 3

Pre-dawn!

The coming-toward-us
Of the Transforming-that-is-not yet-in-power

Presence in the world's becoming
   which we don't control
      nor would want to

   developing
      not made to our order

   about to break out in power
      addressing itself directly to us

A freshly possible
   which we ought not profane or evade
      but tune into

World mood and momentum have started
   toward our Eucharist.

# 10.

# Celebration
# Has Significant
# Form and Vitality

Celebration involves not only awakening, but formings.

If contemporary celebration is the mobilizing and culmination of all arts into a communal art, then the pattern of such celebration must itself be significant form.

The design must express the forming energies of the experience being arted. And done so excellently that the celebrants carry away a residual taste of the quality energy which was forming the celebration, plus a grasp of the overall structure and organizing image.

There is no one ordering of all celebrations.

But on the other hand, we can see three major styles. These may be stated as—

1. Celebration as self-propelling spontaneities achieving significant form as they go along
2. Celebration as a drama of transformations
3. Celebration as growing humanization—itself the culmination of all arts.

These we will now try to develop in successive chapters.

They are not mutually exclusive. And in all three, the question is, Since significant form is important, how does it come about? We become self-conscious that we are engaged in a work of art, and so ask what the guiding sensitivities are.

Some preliminary looking at possible ways of organizing will therefore be of help to us in the designing of all three styles.

## PATTERNS IN WELL-LIKED ART FORMS

Usable clues on designing the pattern of a celebration can be found in typical overall patterns of our best-liked poems, music, contemplative literature. Some most general patterns are—

> 1. *The flowering of a seed into full maturity.* "First the blade, and then the ear, Then the full corn shall appear."
>
> This developmental mode of organization often begins with a memorable image and climaxes at the end by a return to the beginning; now reseen, restated with new significance. Or—as in myth—the essential story may be repeated in different form three times.
>
> A variation of the "awakened seed" line of organization is organization by journey. The celebration takes the form of successive stages of a forceful story—a memorable journey that goes on into horizon.
>
> Another variation follows a prevalent understanding of the creative act—and is closely related to *Gestalt* method of achieving significant form. We begin with a vague, diffuse feeling—a dissatisfaction, an upset,

157

an unease, some beginning to stir within us. Finally, intense feeling takes over, a curve of melody flows into a *line* of melody. The artist with the necessary skills lets it improvise itself into spontaneous forms and utterances. Finally comes the *construction*—a *well*-designed expression possible because of all the previous expressions. And this is so well done that it is memorable.

2. *Center to part, back to center to new part, etc.*

This is Paul's method in writing the book of Romans. He has a compelling experience (of freedom), he reports it, symbolizes it in one striking image, then develops a line of thought and implication. Then comes back to the central experience, only to go off into developing another implication.

This mode might also be called "flower with petals" organization. The center is already discovered and established, but new territories are being taken over and developed, and then back to celebration of the original start.

The poem with an enveloping image which coheres all that is said, in which each stanza pulls in a new field of objects and experience yet also reaffirms the fundamental image or metaphor, would be in this mode of organization. The pattern of a litany is perhaps the clearest illustration of such a style.

3. *Development by dialectic.*

Contrasting movements jam against each other, followed by some sort of resolution. Deeper vision comes out of conflict. Mating of othernesses and metaphors produce new life. Opposing or previously unconnected thoughts reach an overwhelming answer. A constricting viewpoint is broken open, and a range of possibilities appears.

4. *Mosaic* . . . out of which the participants are to make up their personal celebration. Or "chaos" presentations whose purpose is to break up all existing modes of organization in the minds of those present, destroy all existing interpretations and comfortable feeling. This may be meant to be the first step toward new organization—or an end in itself.

## *GESTALT* ORGANIZING FOR EMERGENCE

*Gestalt* psychology offers a complementing and fascinating picture of *how organization comes about*—out of a field of tensions an insight emerges, takes on strength and form, thrusts its quality and power into many areas.

The *Gestalt* mode of organizing for the arousal and perfecting of new patterns of energy can also be stated in the form of principles—

1. Start on the perceptual level: immediate firsthand experience.
2. Tensions are that without which nothing happens.
   Yeasty ferment of interacting insights and experiences
   A field of forces darting into one another
3. A suddenly felt "organizer" erupts: whooshes the field into vivid patterning.
4. Swing it: get rhythm.
5. Get background. Get figure and focus. Get contrast. Let it flow into surrounding territory.
6. Style it.
   In the *organization* lie the meaning and success.

159

## HOW TO HELP AN EXPERIENCE
## DEVELOP ITS MEANINGS

Either by ourselves or in dialogic conversation, we can begin to establish pattern and celebrative energies by working through the following sequence* of helping an experience develop its meaning and flower into celebration.

I. A fresh awareness of what was present in the experience.

Once more see . . . hear . . . undergo the experience.

a) What was the energetic factor that was determining the shape of the experience? The pivotal organizer?

b) The complexity of valuings and feelings present?

The most intense feeling . . . as now felt.

c) What was my intent? The project of my life in that lived moment?

Express in not only verbal, but in nonverbal forms (movement, sound and curve of melody, beat and rhythm, color, design of lived space).

II. Try out words, phrases, imagery . . . with which I can present to myself "It was this kind of experience," "this is how I comprehend it."

a) Compare it to another experience and see what happens.

"This was like ⎯⎯⎯⎯⎯⎯⎯⎯⎯⎯
⎯⎯⎯⎯⎯⎯⎯⎯⎯⎯⎯⎯⎯⎯⎯⎯."

(E.g., "Trying to walk on that icy street yesterday, with leather soles.")

*Based on three steps of phenomenologizing.

160

b) Words and phrases that come up in my mind that might be relevant. Let them dialogue with the experience. Particularly a word or phrase very important in my system of meaning.

c) The *human cry* I hear within the experiencing.

d) The *possibility* trying to have a chance to grow up.

III. *Significance*

a) Is there here a glimmer of a great way of being-in-the-world? Of what makes the human? Of what I'm part of?

b) What do I now affirm? How best say it? To whom?

c) Anybody else ever state these two in beautiful form that also had strength?

## FORMINGS FROM CHRISTIAN ENERGIES

If, as we stated in an earlier chapter, celebration's energies are characterized by freshness, immediacy, hilaritas, and consummation; and if further, we sense that primeval Christian energies might help form the celebration emerging out of our particular lived moment or event, then we would again expose ourselves to the fresh modes that are beginning to characterize Christian existence in our time.

Looking at the following chart of "twelve possibles" which represent shifts now going on in Christian interpretation and aliveness might locate what is happening in some vortex of things going on in other people also. And so vitalize, fill out, and lengthen our experience.

**161**

## SHIFTS IN POSSIBILITY

| From | Toward |
|---|---|
| 1. Sheep existence | 1. Be somebody |
| 2. Obey | 2. Expressive spontaneity |
| 3. Live OLD TIME | 3. NEW TIME. Immediacy |
| 4. Be cautious | 4. Risk the worthwhile |
| 5. Shut-upness | 5. A freedom addressing other freedoms |
| 6. Prattle One-way communication | 6. Communication Two-way |
| 7. Remain hidden | 7. Become manifest |
| 8. Let people get wounded Then pick them up | 8. Create culture and society |
| 9. Lonely individualism | 9. Christ takes form in a band of persons |
| 10. "You ought to" Rage—"Pretend" love | 10. "Caring-for" thinking |
| 11. Christ up in heaven | 11. Only in the midst of the world is Christ, Christ |
| 12. Peace is sunset over a calm lake | 12. The peace of Christ—to which we are called in the one body |

## THE CONTRIBUTION TO ORGANIZING CELEBRATION OF AN UNDERSTANDING OF WHAT LITURGY IS

We are now face to face with the fact that every celebration —in a hidden or open way—is located in some movement of life, some distinctive people who are members one of another, have preferred "great ways of being in the world" and life worlds within which they are existing themselves. We are always part of some cluster of personal energies, thinking and feeling within some small or large culture. When we recognize this, we face liturgy.

162

A working grasp of what might be broadly meant by "liturgy" is an important resource for those leading and constructing celebration.

> A liturgy is the dependable working of a People who believe in one another and in something together.
>
> Having discovered—over a length of time—what this working is, they put it in memorable symbolic form.
>
> So their actions are not empty. So they know that this is what they are, and that they are joined with others in affirming and incarnating this way of being. They have not only experienced paradigms of life, they know that they have. They know and celebrate the meaning of life which breaks through to them in these great ways of being-in-the-world.
>
> They reiterate and celebrate this life again and again.
>
> This affirmed, celebrated, meaningful "working" finally saturates their bloodstream and neurons so that it becomes their effortless style. They possess it at both the conscious and preconscious levels. And it is a social, not merely a personally private thing.

The moment we become a people—a society distinctive and of somewhat enduring character—rather than a conglomerate of alienated ones in pursuit of loneliness and resentment, we have a vital design of life which will be present anytime we celebrate communally. This vital design of life is liturgy—both in incarnate and symbolic form.

For, most essentially, a liturgy is not repetitive rigidities whose magic we will lose if we do not follow them exactly in order and impose them upon all moving experiences. Liturgy is a fresh—but characteristic—working of God's people.

Celebrative liturgy is an "arting" of a People's enterprise with God and man—*existentially* ordered. An immediacy of God's continuing yet often unexpected creations with us, whose parts are not necessarily always in the same sequence or expressed by the same words and acts.

And so it breaks out in different forms and timings. But is still the essential story and song.

We must hold to this essential viewpoint—both for celebration's health and for liturgy's health.

And contemporary celebration, working with immediate experience, new languages and modes of meaning, will be inventing new forms of liturgy as well as vitalizing the existing ones.

But with great concern that they not become "frozen" liturgies. Clichés into which we lapse without thinking or risking, stereotypes which have lost all content and dynamic, prattling which is not the "speaking words" of a virile people, but leisure-time activities of soft affluence.

So in our celebrations, we must get down to the nuclear consciousness which forms our existence, let it have fresh exercise and expression in novel situations.

Without such liturgical quality, celebrations tend to fade off into expressions of a culture religion of masscult, dominated by the latest propaganda slogans and symbolic acts of a secular culture that has lost its sense of Otherness. And so is fad of the year, sentimental kitsch, barbaric in its rage and imprisoned in its loneliness.

Frozen liturgies drive our people to go to such romantic secularisms for their guides to living.

164

The possibility we must choose and develop is to have liturgical quality (an ordering which expresses the fundamental working of the creation in which we participate) without losing the self-propelling ordering of spontaneity freshly acting.

We must have celebration which contains "the poetry of the present" or, in more traditional symbol, which allows the Holy Spirit to have a chance. Partly by not scheduling and forming *everything* in advance, and exclusively as an imitation of what was real on a previous occasion.

But celebration must also have significant form. The *form* of a celebration is crucial—for the *organization and mode of participation in a celebration is its ultimate message.* The structure and tuning of the shaping energies of the celebration are its long term content. The patterned working which distinguishes and forms this particular people, its chief communication.

The specific contents of a celebration are important. But the *journey* (the underlying mode of being in the world) is *most* important. For the journey with which a People is moving puts an envelope around any particular event and gives it meaning. The "liturgy" is a length of functioning by which they can handle the previously unmet and unsolved as well as the familiar encounters of everyday life. Joining in the journey and its constituting consciousness, the celebrants incorporate fundamental style. They become beautifully disciplined spontaneity—simply, directly, and without awkwardness.

To a greater or lesser degree, every celebration presents the consciousness with which this People exists itself and establishes trails through the wilderness of events.

The truly liturgical, then, is a communal experiencing of an overall style of being in the world. It celebrates paradigm and method that transcends every particular moment. Liturgy is

**165**

darting and developing Time—a length of life rather than a sudden bolt out of the unknown. It is a mobilization of constituting consciousness . . . in a precariously becoming and pluralistic world.

So we must keep asking, "What is the working, the walking together, the Story, the myth, the nuclear energies which organize this group's celebration? And does the ordering really lift these up in some unconfused way?"

We are to create new liturgical forms and fresh orders of worship, as well as revitalize those which we have.

### What Is the Life Plot Which Grows a Contemporary Celebration?

If we no longer believe that God is a Caesar or ancient warlord who wants praise, groveling, petition, then these customary activities are no longer the chief work of the people in worship.

If a process God is not primarily one who speaks to us ancient words printed in a book, then contemporary celebration cannot be structured by this assumption.

If God is not one object among other objects but Presence, then his present working—and the working of his people— would be the story which creates a celebration.

The nuclear paradigm for celebrative worhip is *creation and transformation.*

In a becoming universe, there is potential that has not yet been existed. And even though thrown into the world and caught in fate, we still find some space and time in which to live as freedom and generosity. The enactment of such existence would be the structure of celebrative worship.

So we can begin to discern in broadest terms the liturgy which forms a contemporary celebration—*in a particular loca-*

166

*tion, world is being transformed into meaningful world . . .*
*things and events of the world are being taken into the world*
*of the personal . . . persons are awakening . . . a People is*
*emerging.*

To experience, sense, feel such a plot to life is the nucleus
with which contemporary celebration develops its journey and
patterns.

To truly create artistically and thoughtfully, spontaneously
or over a period of time, the designer of celebration needs to
have his mind saturated with

    —a sense of this plot of "hilaritas life."

    —a multi-seeing of the "arenas" where intense growth
       takes place in the course of celebrating.

## Arenas Where the Action Takes Place

What might be meant by this second resource with which we
order celebration may be understood by comparing it to the
equipment of the improvising singer of folk ballad as set forth
in Albert Lord's "Singer of Tales."

The singer of tales in the early days of what is now Yugo-
slavia was able to improvise and artistically present his developing story because he had in mind that the celebrative
story of any heroic life clusters in *certain arenas* where decision
and struggle take place.

With these embedded in his mind, he could freely create
and know how to cluster his creating. The arenas where action
clustered in the traditional Yugoslav drama of heroic life were
such things as (1) the king's council to which came news
which required existential discussion, (2) the "letter missive"
mobilizing the necessary forces and telling them what the
campaign was to be and their part in it; (3) the hero's depar-
ture for enemy country—often disguised, often with com-

panions—to rescue someone or win a bride; (4) the recognition scene, where he is recognized by someone—often a person who befriends him; (5) he is thrown into prison; (6) after some time comes the release episode; (7) what he finds when he returns home; (8) return to the land of the prison; (9) sequel—he rescues someone, and/or wins a bride. Given this understanding of the places where the crucial action takes place, he is free to create and embellish his particular story.

This description is given not that we should imitate these dramatic arenas in our celebrations, but to stir our imaginations about the equipment necessary for the designer of celebrations. We too need some understanding of where the crucial arenas of the celebrative life are.

In the next chapter we will present the outlines of two celebrations which grew out of quite specific arenas and were formed out of the action which took place there. In the chapter after that, celebration is conceived as a series of transformation episodes. And Chapter 13 sets forward basic movements of humanization as organizers and action clusters for communal celebration.

If we have a feeling for these as necessary places where we take time to develop the fullness of that stage of the event, we will construct adequate celebrations. And we can do it with finesse and freedom. Particularly if at the same time, we keep vivid sense of the animating nucleus (plot) which the celebrative story is.

## EXPLORATION I

O the worship of First Church, Uncorporate
  Is awesome

    Out-of-*this* world          Liturgy!


From the very beginning
It batters its people          To grovel as worms
                               God demands it!
Its people have learned
Not to sing
  The organ          Does it much better.

Nothing
Is happening now
  So the service admires          Archeology

Oh—the worship service
  Has dignity          Ordering Mediocrity

Nothing unprogrammed
No breaking out
No wind in the mulberry trees
  No mulberry trees          No morning.

But it is pretty,
With ornaments, sacred noises
  Cave tricks          Picked up through centuries

No one
Is ever alone
  There is organ, choir          Ministers' drone

The Scripture
Was picked by officials
  Way . . . way . . .          Generations ago.

169

Sheep
look up
  and are fed                         Cornstalks waving on high

The worship
objective and packaged
  By two o'clock passes            Into toilets thither and yon.

Cleansing again
Is not needed (or endured)
  Until seven more days

                        Or forty

The preaching
Is sure-fire formula
  analyze the contemporary
    world of centuries ago

                        17 minutes

  assert there is free
    salvation

                        1 minute

The service is
Word pounding word
  piled up in print                  Gutenberg

The liturgical words—
Especially the prayers—
Are beautiful, sonorous, dull
  Never mistaken                 For words used in living.

O the worship
Of First Church Uncorporate
  Is out-of-this-world            Liturgy

The tone and pulse of its sounds
  Trivial
  Irrelevant                      Drivel!

170

# EXPLORATION II

This day
We lived with history-as-it-is-being-made,
    The decisions of each
    Affected the fate of all

This day
People beyond numbering
Acted out the liturgy of profane man

    While the saints deliberated
        Burly sinners ran the world
    Good people kept their mouths shut, their minds shut, their
    hands shut
        Trivialized the good.
    Arrogance had dominion
        Worms crawled
    Stupidity rushed for destruction
        Man feared to state his truth
    Man was wolf to man
        Tiger, tiger, burning bright
        who shaped thy fearful symmetry?
    Terrorism. The big lie.
        War, war, war.

This day
The liturgy of Christ!

    Walls fell down
        Ghettos fell apart
    Wisdom was at the crossroads
        Truth was well said

171

Originality expressed itself
   Fidelity made a gift of futures
Differences dialogued
   Communication was worldwide
Persons chose to bear even more than their share of responsibility and the world's suffering
   When slandered
      we tried to conciliate
   When persecuted
      we endured
"I was not born to share in hatred
   but to share in love."

172

# 11.

# Spontaneities
# Move Experiences
# into Celebration

This style particularly fits a small group of people—possibly not more than forty. They have been through struggle, battle, brought off an enterprise. And now they celebrate. They voice their concerns, the existence questions pressing them. In its freest form the celebration becomes as it happens.

The celebration is a flowing spontaneity of what is interactively awakened in those present. Nobody is trying to impose upon it a form, though by mutual tuning and congruence of intensity, a patterning of flights and perchings emerges. Often the culminating is a total upheaval of informal joyousness. At its best, this is a most authentic celebration and has inherent self-forming organization of meaningful life world and lived moment. And all present have participated in forming. At its worst, its formlessness and meager significance resemble a decaying jellyfish. Whose repetition finally becomes boring, and ends people's desire for celebration.

But this style of celebration—in its better forms—is clear

witness to the fact that the one necessity of all design is the *pulse*, rather than a set of principles or an outline already in the mind to which everything must be shaped. And a pulse grows as any total world grows—according to the ways of creation, letting each vital part affect the total growing.

To some degree every celebration must make use of this style and authenticity of origin. But most celebrations will combine expressive spontaneity with considerable pre-design and prepared art.

Even the freely developing celebration will be governed by somewhat hidden expectations in everybody's mind of what a celebration is, and how it ought to go. This often tends to limit severely what can happen to what has already happened in other such moments. The people who work together in forming any of the three styles of celebration should have some awareness of a *range* of possible ways in which celebration organizes itself.

## THE INHERENT ORGANIZATION AND PULSE
## PUT INTO EXPRESSIVE ART FORMS AHEAD OF TIME

From almost total improvisation where "it becomes as it happens," we move to consider celebration which takes its organization and momentum from experiences just had, but has taken time to create visual-audio-verbal art forms which say very well what has been going on and what grows out of it. Particularly lifting up and intensifying its significance. The whole experience is looked over, shaken down, put into a design that *authentically* symbolizes what it's all about and focuses a vision of future-past-present within which the group can journey.

The result is *inherent liturgy*. A "working" distinctive of this people that is both spontaneous and the best they have been

174

able to create, given some time to do so. Fresh forms of worship, new orders of liturgy have come out of meeting Christ in the world, and the taking form of a band of persons at some particular spot.

The very nature of celebration calls us to compose pulsing celebration that flows, having moments of good art, yet inviting the relevant creative on the spot so that all present feel in on creating the celebration.

We find ourselves creating such new organisms of celebration whenever as a group we have an experience of some intensity and character, and then try to develop it into celebration true to the "genius" of the original experience. Not that we repeat it chronologically, but rather ask ourselves, "What were the shaping energies of this experience? How now do we re-form them at the new level of religious celebration?"

Such was the case for the two celebrations whose outlines we now examine.

Each of the two celebrations involved the participation of all the group members, and very intense hours of special creation on the part of many small "task forces" creating particular contents they felt they wanted to state. The order was a reflection of the educational design of the whole enterprise of the group and some degree of "wisdomed" theory about celebration.

Neither is a structure which every celebration must have. However the nucleus and journey of one new ordering of celebration is here. A liturgy is here. For the structure of each comes from the workings of a group of very committed people over a period of time. One for an intense week, the other distributed over a period of five weeks.

The first, "We Have Destiny," was a celebration culminating five successive Sunday afternoons and evenings of a cluster of laymen and ministers in proportion of about six to one. We

175

were working on "enabling the congregation to happen." The eight episodes of the celebration gave opportunity to again look at, taste, and focus important new life which we had experienced. So far as possible each episode began with something which had happened. Discovery and communication of a personally held truth was one of the enterprises running through the weeks. Two lived moments were presented by two people, with some opportunity for all to talk in groups of four, and then communal report. The "transforming this lived moment into meanings which we live" was worked on in self-organized groups during the last two hours of the afternoon with spill-over through the dinner hour. The closing song, "Christ Takes Form in a Band of Persons," had climaxed each Sunday's meeting, though each time expressed differently. The battle cry was in the form of banners, prepared by each group during the week before.

It cannot be emphasized too much that (as is true of all celebrations) the verve and authentic feel of this celebration came from the reality of the lived moments of our enterprise through the weeks. We all knew that these things had happened and were possible, because we had all been part of them.

So the eight episodes of this first celebration present the workings of a contemporary Hebraic-Christian people. Together they form a story of creation *now*.

## CELEBRATION
### *"WE HAVE DESTINY"*

I. *Interweaving and vitalizing a network of humanness.*
   The journey we are on . . . the enterprise moving toward destiny which we are.
   The rejoicings and hurtings, concerns, yearnings for transformation, which indwell us.

176

Delight and hilaritas in being "bonded and knit"—
In becoming a cluster of people who believe in one
another and in something together.

II. *The creating, the agony, the destruction of this day in the world.*
And where we are related to it.

III. *A lived moment we have experienced rather intensely.*
Re-lived, re-tasted, put into beautiful and communicative form.

IV. *Transforming this lived moment into meanings which we live.*
The whirl of creating, yearning, expectancy that comes out of it.
The Great Conversation . . . focusing our minds on the things that matter most.

V. *The fundamental plot of life we believe in.*
The Innermost Moving of potential which enables it.
Great incarnations of the game of life . . . persons and event.

VI. *A celebration of "our people."*
Moving through time
Toward a destiny

VII. *Offering and battle cry.*
A timely truth we say with all that we are.
The relationship we treasure above all.

VIII. *Going into journey.*
"Christ takes form in a band of persons . . . in the midst of the world."

In the celebration, "A New American Is Being Invented," the focus was the New Time in which we could place our lives, and the new creation we were beginning to be.

A new future-past-present for our country had been experienced by a week's conference of young people and adult advisors in which they exposed themselves to the new way of being-in-the-world which some black men, some Hispanos, some white men, were each beginning to establish in a particular city. They had listened to and visited with each group, tried to understand its projects and new style—always with the background, "Can I be with it or not?"

A striking feature of this celebration was song and music written the night before and played by an improvised combo composed of the people who wrote the song. It was used at various points in the celebration, quite effectively as a sort of litany response to some of the "we believe in this together." Personal reports of "the vivid thing that happened to me during the week" confirmed all present that their new growing and conviction was not queer, nor did they have to keep it bottled up lest someone would find out and attack them. (Which they knew would happen when they got back home.)

But most importantly, the *present* was in everybody's mind —they were delighting in this particular moment, joying that they had discovered and exprienced that the humdrum, partially evil and sick world was being transformed into meaningful world, that events and impersonal things of a city were being taken into the world of the personal, that some few persons were awakening, and a people of the future was emerging of which they were a part.

## CELEBRATION
### "A NEW AMERICAN IS BEING INVENTED"

I. *This day in the whole world.*

II. *Future struggling to be born among us . . .* that we have encountered.

How our lives connect with it.
Delight in the new human consciousness.

III. *Great ways of being-in-the-world.*
Vivid experiences we have had . . . which organize this new life.

IV. *The expected biography of a person's one life on earth* . . . who belongs to "my people."
The present white man's story.
The new white man's story.

V. *A vocabulary of the new white man's speaking words* with which he can more productively feel, choose, think, state his identity, highlight the meaning of life.
Where these words are spoken most effectively . . . the difference they make.

VI. *"We believe in this together."*
Fundamental truths and new ideas which enable us to handle many and novel situations, and to say a "nevertheless" to the old.
The myth which describes how new life originates and how the world is brought together.

VII. *The creating which makes possible human beings* . . .
The God with whom we have a long-term engagement.

VIII. *The surge of feeling and intending which we are.*

IX. *Going into future which is even now present in available world.*

These two celebrations are a pattern or model of the working of God's people which might apply in many places. They are inherent liturgy. Their nucleus is "creation." They came out of not just one lived moment, but a length of lived moment.

## EXPLORATION

Of all the experiences you had as part of the grape workers' strike, which is most vivid?

The thing that hit me most was the spirit of the people. They won't be downed any more.

And this is remarkable because they are really very mild people.

When did this spirit come through to you very clear?

A highly respected Mexican—an older man—going home from a strike meeting, was followed by a car which pushed him off the road, and then they beat him up. I got a phone call late, around 11:30—I was living in a little apartment in a whole row, and was the only one who had a telephone. Everybody just swarmed over to the police department.

The intense feeling that you had was————?

Admiration. Here is a bunch of people that don't have a thing going for them—except what really counts.

It's not merely that they're in need, but they are human dignity.

It's a fantastic human spirit—that "never say die" kind of thing—presented in a humble way. Not cocky, not aggressive.

This is due primarily to this one man Cesar Chavez, or is it part of the culture of these people?

The times, the culture, and the man came together at the right point in history.

You were always a "good guy" with your heart in the right place, but I catch in you now a feeling that your life has a project—and has dimension to it.

Yes, there's more purpose now. And it's not just a long-range thing. There's daily rewards too—working with real people.

When you talk to yourself, do you find yourself using any words out of your religious heritage—or are they all words out of the right now?

> Well, I think "I am come that they might have life, and have it more abundantly."

When your telephone began to ring that night, and you heard what had happened, what words popped up in your mind?

> "Calculated injustice!" It was done deliberately and intentionally.

The human cry that you've heard?

> HELP!

> And then at the time of the big sign-up everyone—growers and workers—felt good. There was good feeling.

It wouldn't be quite "glory, hallelujah"?

> Yes, I think it was. The growers were tired of fighting too. It was hitting them in the pocketbook, but they had been fighting themselves and their consciences too.

So theirs was a cry to be at peace with themselves?

> That wasn't all, but it was there.

How about this cry of human dignity? It's a shout from way down in people, but I hear you saying, "Shouting isn't the way you say it, it's a little more quiet determination."

> I keep hearing marching feet. They started out in Delano, and more people joined in from town to town until when they got to Sacramento, there were 10,000.

Could you put that human dignity into a beat or rhythm?

> Well, it would be sort of like—
> "Now is the tíme
> when we're going to gó, gó, gó
> We're not going to stóp
> We wón't quít.

There was a great way of living that you felt you were part of?

> Cesar Chavez said it about right—

181

When we're really hónest with oursèlves
We must admít that our líves
Are àll that really
Belóng to us.

It is how we úse our líves
That detérmines the kind of mén we áre.

It is my deépest feéling
That to be a mán
Is to súffer
For others.

It is only by gíving our lives
That we fínd life

I am convínced
That the trúest act of cóurage
The stróngest act of mánliness
Is to sácrifice ourselves for óthers
In a totally non-víólent strúggle for jústice

To be a mán
Is to súffer for óthers

God help us to be mén.

—Interview with
Fred Dresser

# 12.

# Celebration Is a Series of Transformations

Celebration can be viewed as a series of transformations. We come out of a celebration freshened, and to some degree a new creature.

The purpose of this chapter is to suggest the occurrence of a series of one kind of transformation:

1. Experiences and world are transmuted into meanings and symbols.
2. Meanings transformed into selfed bodies.
3. Individuals transformed into a People.

Each metamorphosis is into a new mode of being.

Together these three transformations contribute movement and patterning to a celebration. The total pattern of such celebration may be visualized as movement of "spiraling transformations in celebrative life."

The whole series of transformations begins with the lived moment. Everything depends upon beginning here. Lived moment and event are transmuted into name, symbol, meanings

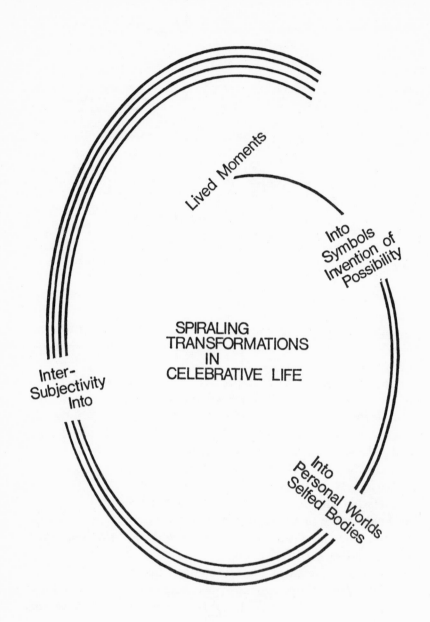

Lived Moments

Into
Symbols
Invention of
Possibility

SPIRALING
TRANSFORMATIONS
IN
CELEBRATIVE LIFE

Inter-
Subjectivity
Into

Into
Personal Worlds
Selfed Bodies

of life, new possibility. With meanings symbolized we can put together future world as well as guide and interpret our present acts. To transmute event into symbols and culture is to arrive at a human level of living.

Transmuting meanings into selfed body and a selfed world is a second great transformation. So that beyond achieving symbol comes the self's fresh incarnation. For unawakened people, words stop at verbal actuality. Such people tend to regard a name or an idea as a label and conversational counter, rather than a statement of "possibility-for-me." To some degree this is true for all of us—particularly since only a few ideas are worthy of completing themselves as burgeoning incarnation into us and our world. But some do have the power of moving into living flesh and pulsing blood. Out of their power —when mated with our existing self—they metamorphose from symbolic world to personal existence world. Into bodied self (or *selfed* body—whichever value we want to emphasize). Into a "worlded" self and a selfed world.

So we come to the third transformation . . . into a People.

Symbols and communication (the first transformation), in combination with *encountered* incarnations (the second transformation), transform us into another mode of actuality—a corporateness of consciousness, an intersubjectivity of persons who have an enterprise moving toward a destiny.

This third transformation is into a world of intersubjects who are on the way to becoming fully personal, yet are also a common field of sensibility, significant symbol, mutual obligations, and rights. This corporateness is more than a system of symbols, or even a styled consciousness within which they can communicate with each other, co-create, and out of which each individual consciousness is birthed and individuated. It is energies and bodies turned into a multiplet of personal centers thrusting into the world.

To describe these three transformations is to make an important statement about the total event which a celebration is. But we must not think of them too ploddingly as a straight-line journey. They are going on all the time, and as they happen in the celebrants.

It seems most profitable to think of them as an evolutionary spiral that not only mounts, but expands outward. (It also has inter-roads across which action travels at unexpected times.) As life goes on, the spiral comes around again and again to the previously established transformations, but each time fresh possibility can emerge.

So in constructing a celebration we can focus on an expanding, partly repeating spiral of transformations—lived moments into meaningful possibility, into fresh existence as person, into intersubjectivity.

Each transformation needs some leisurely chance to grow up past the point of birth . . . else we have the wasteland of a motorized tourist. We should put considerable artistry into clarifying, intensifying and flaming, architecting into beautiful design and strong statement, an important transformation as it occurs.

Transformations offer one possible pattern of a celebration.

And so celebration's myth emerges. A myth presents how life is originated, its contradictions overcome, its partialness and ambiguous mixture transformed into the next stage of life. Anytime, anywhere.

# EXPLORATION

"I was caught up in celebration. And I was present at the making of worlds and the forming of persons.

Lived moments that had not yet found their foundation and form came up through the waters and became good earth. Light shone in darkness, and the darkness could not overcome it.

Stirred by soaring imagination, the prairie of lived moments became forms of word and symbol. Fresh growth of poetry-of-the-present transfigured the bare earth. Colors and textures, forms and rhythms of a universe of meaning firmed up. New possibility became a tree of life within a horizon that vaulted all that had been.

And that was the second day.

And man said, 'Let this seed bring forth much fruit. Let it incarnate in me so that I become manifest in significant form.' And the seed became a selfed body.

And that was the third transformation in creation.

These persons were in encounter, and became a Presence to one another. So that they became energy charged with meaning. They lived in time as Time.

They began to speak with one another, and communed in many ways until they became a body bonded and knit together in a world net covering the earth.

They were song and journey. And a habitat of spirit."

# 13.

# The Culminating Art
# of All Arts

Contemporary communal celebration is the culminating art of all the arts.

Communal celebration mobilizes all the arts, and incorporates their contributions in its own realization.

It also provides a community which receives the most authentic art produced by its members and congruent spirits. So that the artist, who in other eras was forced to subsist upon his own understanding or appreciation by a small tribe, has a reference "field of presence." And even more—now that we are entering upon an era where not only is there being produced art for the millions but everybody is becoming able to get in on the act—we can have a *society of people creating art* with resident vitality. If we accept contemporary celebration as one of our forms of culture!

Contemporary celebration is the culminating art also because it is the widest and deepest mode of consummatory experience. This in itself is high cause for celebrating celebration. How and where else can a whole community establish habits and a "place where" all together they sense deeps and finalities? The memorable flashes of beauty and wistfulness that startle their consciousness, the constant emergings and disappearings that characterize human life? Where else can visions and dreams which stir our imaginations and awaken hitherto slumbering energies be lifted up, put into memorable symbol, treasured, enjoyed as present in the concrete lived moments of our life, their full glory tasted even though we ourselves will always see the Promised Land from a distance? Where else can we together relish the cause we serve, even though we are terribly finite? Where else can we be perfected in faith? Together weave together a story that enables each of us to exist as fullness of Time?

Communal celebration is the consummatory, culminating art of all arts also because it is an art.

A most complex and difficult one—expressing multi-tuned, multi-dimensional multi-spiraling, multi-content consciousness. In the multi-languages now available, and of the intersubjectivity of many people. Celebration is the art of arting communal mind—and by the community. The climactic, enjoyable art of together creating culture.

So we must get on with establishing the sensitivities and principles of such an art. And that is what all this book is about.

But we can also focus in on some quite specific but broad components of communal celebration as art form. *The movements of humanization are also the art principles of the complex art of communal celebration.*

We can begin to understand such a statement by using an analogy. As we look at paintings, we begin to understand that important components of the art of painting are how the artist arranges and executes darks and lights, lines and movement, nuances and patterns of colors and what they do to one an-

189

other, textures and brush strokes, lived space, pervading feeling tone. These are components of the art of painting.

Even so, the art of communal celebration is composed of five fundaments—worlding, interweaving and interiorizing, lived moment burgeoning, selves transforming, peopling.

These are the complex artistry in which the artist in celebration must be trained—along with the more specific visual, audio, and verbal arts. If any of these arts is weak, we cripple celebration.

## THE ART OF WORLDING

"Worlding" is a necessary act—particularly for *contemporary* celebration. A celebration must give us a world and force us to locate ourselves in it. So that we can be a self-in-world rather than a nothingness. So that we can understand and correctly treasure some lived space where we have being, and know that we do.

Celebration does not take place in ether, nor do we. Unless this worlding is done excellently, we have violated one of the fundamental arts of communal celebration, even though we may mobilize many audio and visual arts.

Essentially worlding is a psychological art—the artful way people perceive what has to do with them, and simultaneously form a self-in-*world*.

Some of the components of this process we know.

A high state of vigilance (energies partly mobilized, partly loose), of alertness, of realization that *life-death* world is about to appear—is much of any person's power to form life worlds. What is the art of awakening such a state?

A person's sense of "I AM", his self-identity, his respect for himself and confidence that he can bring himself off, the feedforward of a project—all are part of the powers of worlding.

190

How are these sensings and momentums awakened so that worlding may be *well* done?

To be present where other people are clarifying, intensifying, putting into forceful form a life world, gives us a vicarious experience of the art of worlding. The process is set in motion within us as we hear and see other people voicing their perceiving of world, their journey into it, their interiorizing and valuing.

Worlding is especially fascinating when a world takes on form right before our eyes—as contrasted with a presented fixed world that has no surprises and no becoming. A world leaping with the poetry of the present invites us into getting inside it, and letting it get inside us.

A high sense of actuality is another part of the art of worlding. The reports and reporters of world must be felt to be credible witnesses. Believable both in their honesty and in the fact that they were there. Only the direct, raw real—rather than the smoothed over product of somebody's mind—upsets us into creating self-in-*world*.

### INTERWEAVING
### INDWELLING

Interweaving-interiorizing is likewise artistic action which encompasses many arts. But also has its own basic principles.

The interweaving of those present into a network of humanness is felt as a resonance that permeates the celebrative group and seems to fill the whole room.

An appreciative feeling ripples through the whole congregation that other people are being awakened as feeling, enjoying persons. People are no longer staring but participating. The look out of their faces and eyes, the warmth of their voices, invites dialogue. A mood is established that we are enjoying together something that only that special moment can create. People are together *inside* an experiencing. Its vibrations are awakening others as well as themselves, so they are among human beings.

Something is running toward me and into me from the others, and from me toward and into others. And together we know that this is happening. We believe that the others are trying for integrity, do not want to live duplicitously. That they are honestly presenting how it is with them, rather than playing games with us, mouthing words that are not their speaking words. We recognize one another as bearing goodwill and wishing well to one another. Persons are being drawn toward others. Something of others begins to dwell in each of us—and we like it.

What had been an assembly becomes a *live* "congregation" —for something has been set in motion in each person present (at least those next to us), and *all know that it has.*

Almost everyone senses that a cluster is being established of people who accept one another as *fully* human.

How does this resonance come about? By celebrative existence on the part of the leaders of the celebration? How do people come to feel that the person next to them is stirring with similar resonance? That something of themselves has been interiorized by at least some people present? That an experience of theirs calls out resonance in somebody else? That something of them is in the celebration?

All the skills of communication are relevant in this art. Communicating—not information or instruction—but a style of consciousness, a preferred way of being-in-the-world, potent energies. How is a *person* communicated? Perhaps by hearing his inner speech, i.e., what he says to himself in his own heart when he is struggling with his destiny, and not trying to im-

192

press or influence anybody. Perhaps the vocalization of inner speech is a critical factor in celebration?

What is the art of celebration's interpersonal events? How do we (and all others present) possess these—not as rules and wooden directions on what we ought to do, but as instant sensitivities, relevant expressive spontaneity? Beautifully and powerfully being as a corporateness.

## LIVED MOMENTS BURGEONING

The art of "lived moments burgeoning" develops as we understand the process of all organic growth by awakened seeds. It might be called development art. Which is another name for dynamic organization—not as imposed from without, but as the pushing up through the ground of a determined, awakened seed on its way to realizing its nature.

"Lived moments burgeoning" is also transformation art. The art of metamorphosing events and things of the world into personal consciousness. We must learn the disciplines of phenomenologizing!*

## SELVES TRANSFORMING

Transformations and recenterings of the energies of the Self have been a persistent event in the long course of Christian experiencing—symbolized vividly by Paul's transformation scene while on the road. Conversion of the divided self into a new "model" and empowering of new life has been a peak experience in Christian celebration. We do not know very well its contemporary forms. Nor do most church worship services expect it to happen. Compared with this goal, church services are pleasant leisure-time activities.

Of all the arts, we know least about the art of nurturing tre-

*Work up your own "lived moment art" as you live the possibilities of processing lived moments which are presented in Section IV.

mendous upheaval and reorganization, the relocation of the habitual center of our personal energies. Or even how to firm it up and anchor it in intersubjectivity—provided it does happen! Hopefully, it will always partly maintain itself as Mystery —something we cannot control, but respect and invite on its own terms. But it is a great art, perhaps the consummation of all arts. For it is the awakening of spirit.

## PEOPLING

Peopling is the art of politics—in the deepest and best sense of that term. Constituting a city which has citizens and foundations. Writing history with *living* documents, rather than with words on a page.

Peopling is the emergence of a "breakthrough community" which has an epiphany. And now believing in one another and in something together, is moving toward incarnation of the highest and best.

Peopling is pilgrim feet striding through a wilderness, forming an enterprise moving through time, causing things to happen now. The critical factor in peopling is a Joshua calling to the assembly, "Choose you this day whom you will serve, . . . but as for me and my house we will serve the Lord." (24:15 RSV.)

Peopling is bringing about common fate situations—where all know that none will be saved or grow unless all are saved and grow.

Peopling is the emergence of significant symbol out of the sharing of experiences and convictional beliefs by many people until they have created together a meaningful home. So that they are no longer strangers and foreigners, but a habitation of God through the spirit.

Peopling is the culmination of celebration.

## EXPLORATION

As I walk through the wildness of this world
It is crammed with good men, and men barbarians to one
    another
Each shouting he is totally right
And should rightfully destroy all the others
      I am but one small man
      And the timing is fast and short

Often I am wit's end, perplexed
How understand such a world, let alone take hold of it?
Hunted, struck down, defeated
      I may not be much
      But the cause I serve has greatness

"I fight till my sword becomes part of my hand
And when they are joined together as if the sword grew out
    of my arm
And the blood runs through my fingers
Then I fight with the most courage"
      The odds are the underdog's
      If future is on his side.

Everything I do is mixed with imperfection, estrangements
But I have appeared, formed some beauty
Shaped worlds for some others to live with me
Done the best I could . . . given this time, strength, and the
    resistance to it.
      Exulting and despairing
      Warmth and a chilly cold

*Nothing* remains solved
Out of each victory and defeat come new opportunities

Also new disasters, problems. And ultimately
Death takes me down to defeat
    Life is in the *being*.

All living is moving in the dark, with the help
Of the once-in-awhile shine-through in some opening between
    clouds.
But to find more truth
We must move with the truth we presently see
    The light we see routs some darkness

We do not place ourselves in a world to have pleasure
But to become Man
Share in the passion and action.
Once you feel the depth, it is firm
    For New Time is stirring
    And we can live within it

We are to be heard
We will be felt
    For the possible which we see
    Seems to us momentous

       *   *   *   *   *   *

# VI  WITH WHOM, THEN, CAN WE DEVELOP CELEBRATION?

# 14.

# Where Would You Go?

I would go to a meeting of persons where there was enough flow of honest feeling to wash out the grimy dirt and monotonous sameness of my own limited feelings. To a meeting that had honest, headlong vitality. And I met the real.

I would like to be in a place where people are *freshly being*. Where some things are happening for the first time. Yet I feel at home. There's enough familiar that I feel—

"Here is my territory, my kind of people, a fit home for my ventures into existence. The kind of person I crave to be is going on here.

Here is the pulse of growing—rather than deadness. Once in awhile—at least—a tumultuous tide comes in. Once in awhile—after a drive up a steep and winding road—a horizon opens a world we hadn't seen before."

I would like to be part of a meeting of people who are beginning to believe in one another, and in something together. So their life has style. They invent enterprises worth pouring energies into. There's something their life is about and for. And that something has a future.

Which brings me back to the main point—these people are dealing with the real.

And with possibility-for-me.

With whom then can we develop celebrations?

With persons and groups who—

Are in meaningful time, rather than clock time
    Sensing the future that is present even now
    Tuned with expectancy . . . toward being resolute

Have lived moments
    Aware of the tremulous presence and coming of the
        kingdom of God.

Enjoy making culture and history, rather than just consum-
    ing them.
    Not afraid to stand up and out.

Delight in significant form
    Are artists and theologians . . . even though amateur
    Can receive the instress of an inscape
    Once in awhile are lost in awe, wonder, contempla-
        tion

Come alive in the interpersonal and the intersubjective.
    Enjoy conversation that reveals
    Not individualistic, alien, arrogant . . . but swimming.

Are capable of deep feeling

Just folks like the rest of us when we are not turned in upon
    ourselves.

The socially creative person and the celebrative person are
    properly identical.

The one aspect will not grow without the other.

# EXPLORATION I

Within doublemindedness
    Man is not at one with himself
With commitment only to a certain degree
    He is nothing definite

He learns and learns
    Yet never comes to a knowledge of truth
He forgets the most important of all
    To support justice in the service of truth

Is your mind continually divided
    Because you wish to be in harmony with the
        crowd?
By your silence . . . are the circumstances
    Still more unfavorable to the truth?

        All depends upon this
            Your own decisive activity!
        Only he knows the truth
            Who participates in the truth! [1]

---

[1] Arranged from Kierkegaard's *Purity of Heart Is to Will One Thing.*

# EXPLORATION II

Tune: Foundation

There is no well-marked road which our history will take
It turns, writhes, and darts with surprise unforeseen
Creation still moves through travail and through mirth
And justice, like waters, keeps fresh'ning the earth.

We walk with a truth that is ever before
And sing the Lord's song in an ever strange land
Man's life is a mountain with valleys between
And spiraling paths through the mixed-up ravines.